MARKHAM ROBERTS

NOTES ON DECORATING

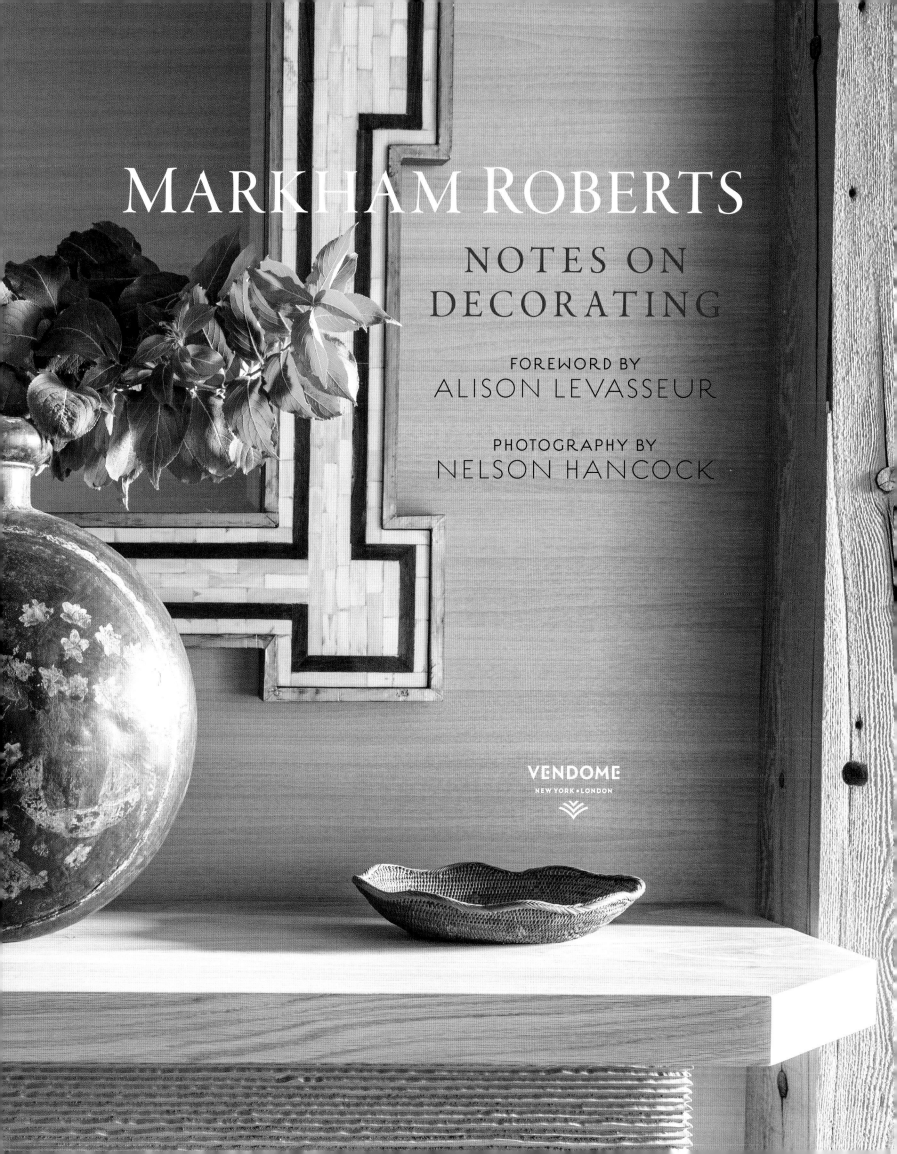

MARKHAM ROBERTS

NOTES ON
DECORATING

FOREWORD BY
ALISON LEVASSEUR

PHOTOGRAPHY BY
NELSON HANCOCK

VENDOME
NEW YORK • LONDON

CONTENTS

FOREWORD BY ALISON LEVASSEUR 13

INTRODUCTION 15

THE CLIENT'S POINT
OF VIEW 21

A SENSE OF PLACE 55

PRACTICALITY 113

LAYERING AND
EMBELLISHING 151

SOMETHING DIFFERENT
OR UNEXPECTED 183

THE FATES 227

THE EVOLUTION
OF A HOUSE 259

ACKNOWLEDGMENTS 295

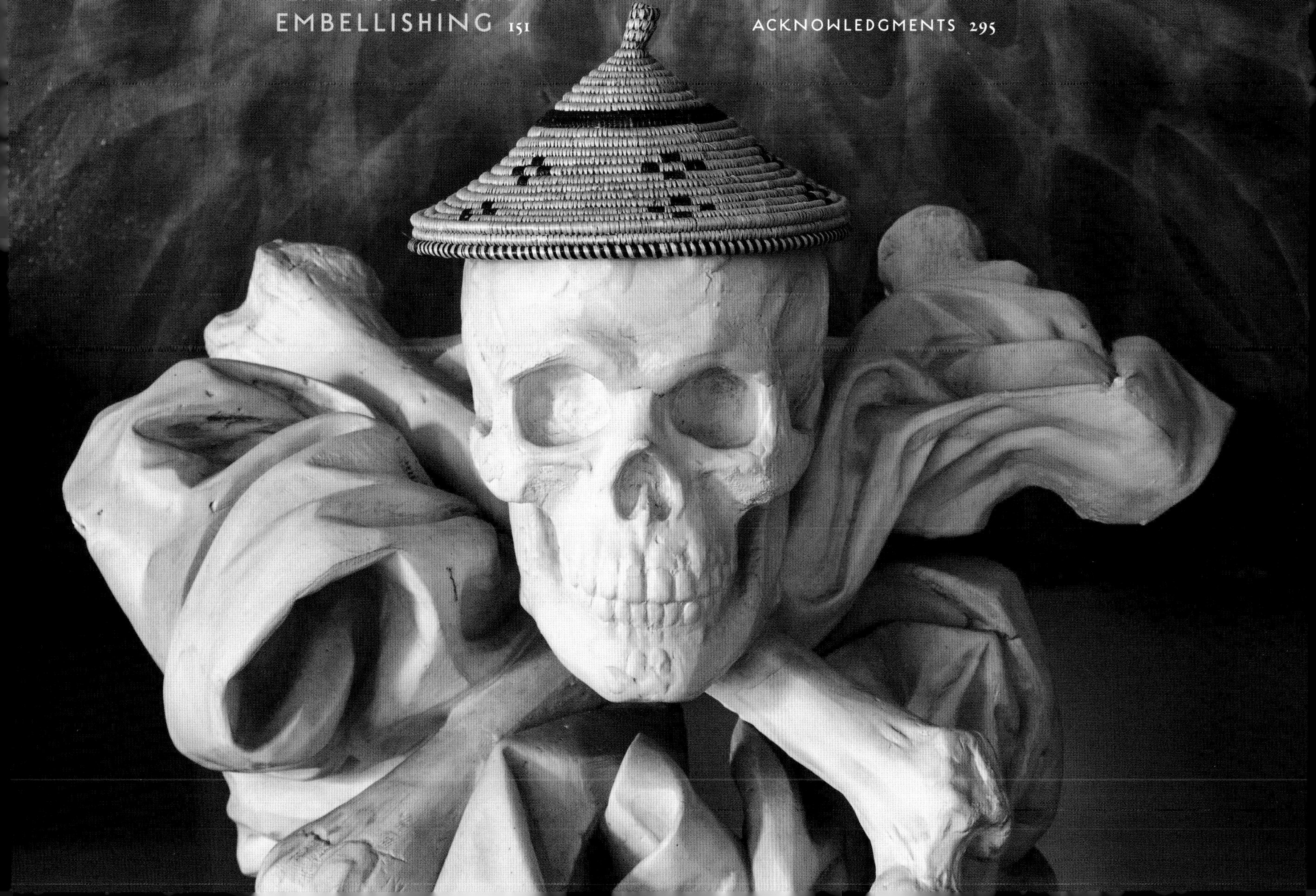

FOREWORD

ALISON LEVASSEUR

GREAT AMERICAN DESIGN HAS ALWAYS ROAMED the globe—and the centuries—deriving inspiration wherever it is to be found. In drawing on the aesthetic traditions of ancient Greece and Rome, the Far East, eighteenth-century Europe, and many other cultures and epochs, all-American decorating has embraced versatility, comfort, integrity, and an overall optimism.

Since launching his own firm some twenty-five years ago, my dear friend Markham Roberts has continued that dialogue with periods and places, always with impeccable flair. Thoroughly considered—but never overthought—his rooms reveal the things he loves: a quilt thrown casually across a skirted table, a chartreuse parasol hung upside down to form a light fixture, and books everywhere. Markham is as comfortable with a valuable antique as he is with a catalogue find. Look closely at a shelf and you may spot a toy dinosaur, a Rubik's Cube, or a vintage Pez dispenser standing next to an eighteenth-century gilt-bronze-mounted Chinese vase. Beautiful and interesting objects of any provenance can bring him pleasure.

It's no wonder that legendary interior designer Mark Hampton scooped Markham up when he was in his early twenties, a recent graduate of Brown working in client services at Sotheby's. Hampton recognized in Markham something the future designer hadn't yet seen in himself and gave him six years of mentorship, which taught him that the decorating business is more than just pretty curtains and pillows (even though Markham certainly has a playfully sophisticated way with pattern and color). I can think of no better school.

Though such luck has played a part in his career, in Markham's case there's also a tremendous amount of hard work, balanced by boundless creativity. He identifies his grandmother as the person who first showed him what a home can and should be. And his Midwestern roots, as the map of Indiana hanging prominently in his office makes abundantly clear, remain a point of pride. That honesty, integrity, and charm are all very much part of what attracts people to him. Loyal, confident, charismatic, and always an attentive listener, he tailors each project to the needs and desires of his clients, many of whom are generations of the same family. His projects range widely in style and location, from an elegant London townhouse to a grand Park Avenue apartment for a notable American heiress, from a richly layered family house in Greenwich, Connecticut, full of Old World glamour to a warm Montana ski retreat, from a chic Manhattan apartment for young, sophisticated art collectors to a dazzlingly eclectic house in Beverly Hills.

At *Architectural Digest*, we have had the pleasure of publishing several of Markham's projects. A seaside house on Nantucket remains one of my favorites. With layers of floral fabrics and cheerful painted floors, it's quintessential Markham and a classic American beauty. His own country house in Clinton Corners, New York, and his retreat in Port Townsend, Washington, both show that he is comfortable in his own skin—and his rooms reflect that ease. When selecting projects for publication, we gravitate toward places that bring us joy. For me, these houses truly deliver.

Last July, much to my delight, Markham joined me on a field trip to one of America's greatest houses: Beauport, the summer retreat in Gloucester, Massachusetts, built by the antiques collector and interior decorator Henry Davis Sleeper for himself in the early twentieth century. Despite a heat wave, Markham arrived with a smile on his face and his eyes and mind wide open. Wandering through the house, he had an immediate grasp of the labyrinth of rooms, marveling at the collection of amber glass and the celadon Zuber wallpaper, with its hand-painted scene of birds and branches. His enthusiasm is always electrifying.

Like Sleeper, Markham is a scholar and a collector, masterful at creating interiors that feel relevant and authentically inhabited. Like Beauport, which evolved over several decades, Markham's own seaside house in Port Townsend has been years in the making, its daring mix of fabrics and rattan only improving with time. Both houses hark back to a spirit of optimism that is the essence of American decorating. Sleeper laid the foundation, Hampton mastered the art, and Markham upholds and updates the tradition. As this book—which is full of practical advice, inspiring beauty, and more than a little humor—makes clear, he continues to reward us with rooms that look and feel good. What could be more American than that?

INTRODUCTION

Though I suspect that most people will pay more attention to the pictures in this book than to the words I've written (I have been accused of droning on by my editor, among others), it is a pleasure and certainly a privilege to be able to express my thoughts and insights about the job I love. Getting to write a second book is really the icing on the cake. In the first book I laid out my approach to the basics of decorating; in this one I focus on some of the more subjective and particular aspects of my work.

I've said it before: decorating is a complex business and process. Our job is to help our clients achieve a result that will give them immense pleasure, yet with all of the intricacies of different minds looking at the same thing, we run the risk of getting the opposite reaction from the one we intended—disappointment. There are thousands of moving parts that need to come together cohesively for a successful outcome. So at the start of every project, I try to glean as much information as I can from clients about what I call their decorating hopes and dreams. I look to clients to help me determine the direction of the design. Understanding their point of view is the subject of my first chapter. My goal for each project is for it to reflect the clients' aesthetic or lifestyle, rather than one I have imposed on them.

In my work as a decorator, I wear many hats and have to consider many topics. Thinking practically may not be the first thing that one associates with decorators, but practicality is very much on my mind and plays a large role in designing successful rooms. It is equally important to take into account the location or sense of place of each project. Knowing what elements are appropriate for a house in the mountains versus a house at the beach is key. An African mask or an Amish basket can work in an urban apartment, for example, but a seashell or coral theme would be a little odd in a landlocked place like, say, Montana or the Midwest.

In another chapter I discuss the effort I make to do something different in my designs. I'm good at mixing patterns and colors in unexpected ways, for instance, and I think this gives my projects at least some aspect of originality. I also put a lot of thought into designing custom furniture for my clients because I think that creating unique pieces helps make each job special, rather than cookie-cutter or clone-like, as much decorating can seem. My clients appreciate the extra effort, and it makes the work much more fun and interesting for me.

Though I have been in this business for a long time, it is still immensely gratifying to have clients who really want to work with me. They not only place their trust in me but also, and more importantly, often really indulge my creativity, even if they can't necessarily envision what I have in mind at first. I devote one of the chapters to a single project for a client who was particularly willing and ready to let me have at it to make something unique and completely suited to her.

Decorating isn't always a matter of finishing a project and stepping away. Often, we are called upon to return to projects and adapt our work to reflect changing circumstances in life. In the last chapter, I focus on my partner James's house in the Pacific Northwest and discuss how it has evolved over time. Decorators need to be flexible (except, perhaps, when confronted with hideous possessions or particularly bad ideas). Our purpose is to help our clients, so if we can continue to look at things in different ways and learn, then we are much more likely to be successful at realizing our clients' goals.

I hope the reader comes away with the sense that I love my job and enjoy creating different atmospheres for very different people in very different places. I don't want to work in the same vein over and over again or force a signature style on anyone. Sure, I am as big a fan of comfort, proper lighting, and functionality as I am of beauty, but I want to stretch myself and help clients stretch too, and make as much as I can out of every project or design challenge.

And decorating can be a CHALLENGE. Dealing with complex, sometimes difficult logistics, working around people's

feelings and emotions, and easing people through construction or moving is not for the faint of heart. Yes, much of my job is fun—especially at the end, when the design becomes a reality. But there is so much more to the business of decorating, as I referred to it in my first book. And like any job, decorating is full of hassles and frustrations and the hard work to get every aspect of the job at hand done. Decorators have to pay attention; they have to be consultants, salesmen, ambassadors, therapists, and responsible financial managers. It's a lot to think about and a lot to shoulder. Humor gets me through much of the difficulty encountered on the job, just as it does in life. I try to keep things light and fun whenever possible. I don't take myself too seriously, and I look for clients who don't either.

I am lucky to have the opportunity to work with a wide range of people—American and foreign, young and old, formal and casual—the majority of whom are sophisticated and interesting, funny and charming. I often have to travel out of town to meet with potential clients and have a look at the projects to see if we should embark on working together. And when they inevitably ask what I might need for my visit, I send the following set of ridiculous demands just to test the waters. I find that most clients appreciate levity. One client in particular responded to my joke directives by hiring me on the spot, even before we met in person. She said she had already told the other "pompous" decorator whom she had interviewed that she was going in another direction—mine, thankfully, and we've had a grand time working together ever since.

MARKHAM'S TRAVEL NEEDS

I prefer my bedroom temperature to be maintained at 69 degrees F. during the day, with a gradual decrease down to 60 degrees over the course of the night. And I like water to be placed within 2 feet of the bed—either Poland Spring or NYC tap water from the Upper East Side. I prefer white sheets, ironed, and a medium-weight duvet folded in half at the end of the bed. Also I need a 150-watt, 3-way soft Edison bulb in the bedside lamp and an Itty Bitty book light left in the bedside table drawer, if possible. I sleep best with the rainforest sounds of a noise machine. Please wake me by ringing a small bell outside my bedroom door at 8:30 AM before turning on any of Beethoven's piano sonatas or any of the Mozart piano concertos—I'm not picky. My bath should be drawn at 8:45 AM and filled with a ratio of ⅔ hot water, ⅓ tepid water. And then I take breakfast of crisp bacon and 2 soft scrambled eggs with buttered toast back in bed, which I prefer to have been changed and made while I'm in my bath.

PAGE 1: Wall upholstery of simple ticking, with the stripes set in varying directions and matched perfectly, creates handsome paneling in this Nantucket dining room, and likely drove the installers to drink.

PAGES 2–3: The fine eighteenth-century Georgian marble mantel, a wedding gift to my clients from the wife's father, was moved from their former London house and now anchors the pared-down, modern architecture of the entrance hall in their new house, warming guests upon arrival. The snake photograph by Guido Mocafico may have the opposite effect.

PAGES 4–5: The old hayloft of the nineteenth-century carriage house in the Hudson Valley is now my working studio in the country. As a bonus, when guests (or my partner, James) prove exhausting, our dog, Harriet (Harrie), and I can escape to it.

PAGES 6–7: Floral and geometric patterns in rich, saturated colors give this Nantucket living room its visual impact, but the subtle use and display of the client's fascinating collections make the eye wander across every surface.

PAGES 8–9: A painted and hammered nineteenth-century Indian copper water vessel, or moon flask, found its way to this ski house in the mountains of Montana and holds court on the custom-carved and -ribbed entry hall console. I asked the client if she could keep whiskey in it to revive me after arduous hikes.

PAGE 10: This beautiful painting of the moon by South African artist Kurt Pio hangs above a custom settee in the billiard room of a house in the mountains. It gives me the bragging rights to say I hung the moon.

PAGE 11: In the front parlor of our country house, the memento mori skull, from a sale of Fred Hughes's possessions, serves to remind me to use my time on earth wisely, while the mandala painting by Julia Condon behind it makes me ponder the wondrous geometry of the universe. Deep thoughts!

PAGE 12: In the dining room of our house on Puget Sound, an eighteenth-century watercolor of a gull by Dutch artist Aert Schouman hangs above a nineteenth-century Portuguese Palissy ware plate depicting crabs and other sea creatures. The painting on the console, by artist Anthony Prud'homme, visually echoes the cuttings from the garden that I bring inside.

PAGE 14: In my study at our house in the country, the Deco writing table by De Coene and the canvas work bags around it may look burdened with responsibility, but everything in the room makes me happy and placates any desire to be away from my desk. The late nineteenth-century painting of the Temple of Philae by American artist Edwin Blashfield reminds me of drifting up the Nile.

PAGE 16: Harriet watches me climb the stairs to the loft of my carriage house studio, which I renovated to be an office in the country. A Carlo Nason bubble lantern hangs above a nineteenth-century English leather-topped partners desk.

PAGE 17: My work table, seemingly always full, has a plain, still unfinished wooden top. The base is a giant burled tree trunk that I found years ago at the Nashville Antiques & Garden Show and had long held in storage.

WHETHER CLIENTS HAVE A STRONG POINT OF view or I am helping them to form one, the single most important consideration for a new project is to glean how clients really want to live. Some come with lots of baggage—the good kind, like art collections and beautiful things—for me to incorporate. Others are decorating a second home or starting fresh. Whatever the case, I always look at their lifestyles: Do they have kids or dogs? Do they like to entertain or prefer to hole up in front of the TV or with a book? And what are the most important things they want out of their new surroundings?

Decorating isn't always a big, complete job. I am often called upon to help friends and clients in some smaller way—to assimilate inherited pieces into their lives, to rethink and weed out old possessions, or to change a child's room into an office for gleeful empty nesters. If I weren't able to understand their different points of view and goals, these relationships would never last.

The owner of the beautiful London house on pages 20–31 has been a close friend since college, and I have always admired her taste. I had decorated a lovely summer house for her family on Long Island, but getting to help them move from a big house on a fancy square in South Kensington to a cool house in Notting Hill, with a large, beautiful garden and a modern, stripped interior, was a huge treat. The goal was to mix furniture and art I had known and loved from their previous homes with new pieces to create a fresh look. The steel-and-brass neoclassical-style desk and étagère by John Vesey look completely new and chic with the Tuareg matting and the fanciful rug by Allegra Hicks in their respective rooms. With such additions, and from the new ways we grouped and used their existing furniture and art, the result is very much in keeping with the clients' taste but in a less traditional way than before.

In the country house on pages 32–37, which I decorated for clients with Persian, European, and American roots, I mixed diverse furniture, art, and accessories into a distinctly American blend. More than anything, the clients enjoy relaxing with their large family and many friends and guests, so I tried to make the décor flow from room to room and be flexible enough to accommodate any number of people. I also wanted to make it attractive, of course, but I specifically dialed back the decorating to enhance, rather than conflict with, the stunning natural views out of every window. I made use of their accumulated possessions in new and different ways, so that they would see them from a different perspective. Displaying their vast collection of pre-Columbian ceramics, for instance, on the library shelves and around the living room, and grouping their collection of antique

THE CLIENT'S POINT OF VIEW

maps on the walls not only added depth to the decorating but also made it more personal and special.

The glamorous apartment on pages 38–43 was done for one of two famous sisters whom I am lucky and happy to know and work for. This client's sister's beautiful triplex apartment was my very first job when I launched my own firm and is featured in my first book, but I got my hands on this Park Avenue apartment only a few years ago, and it is just the kind of decorating that I was trained to do by Mark Hampton all those years ago. Both sisters have extraordinary works of art, collected over the years and inherited from their renowned family of art collectors and benefactors, and I was thrilled to get to work around all of it. I should point out that the influence of my grandmother comes equally into play in this type of decorating. The rooms are formal yet inviting and quite cozy. Art and antiques take pride of place, but it feels like a comfortable home, rather than a museum or a showplace done just to impress.

Decorating can take time, and sometimes clients need the freedom to proceed slowly. A special client, the spirited younger sister of a friend from college when I first met her thirty years ago and whom we still refer to as the Teen Rebel, grew into a champion mother, tireless philanthropist, and ardent enthusiast of decorating. She very tragically lost a hard-fought battle with pancreatic cancer, but her illness focused all our efforts on making her house a home for her beautiful daughter—one suited to their French and American heritage. The family room on pages 44–45 particularly illustrates the warm and cozy environment I helped her create.

The teal lair on pages 50–53 is a study I did for the famous Kips Bay Decorator Show House one year. It gave me a chance to express my own point of view. We were charged with transforming a room in a challengingly short amount of time, and out of laziness I chose the smallest room in the very grand Beaux-Arts mansion. Most decorators conjure an elaborate or extravagant design theme, like a library for Winston Churchill or a garden room for Bunny Mellon, but I was trying to finish my first book and didn't have much spare time to execute a grand scheme, so I chose to do a small dream study for myself. And I decided to decorate it in the vein of the great French decorator Henri Samuel, whose chic and sophisticated mix of antiques and modern furniture I have always admired. Out of further laziness—and to save time searching for art to hang on the walls—I pilfered art from the walls of our apartment and house in the county. Things looked a little stripped and bare for the duration of the show, but it made my life that much easier. I loved that room and was sad to see it dismantled in the end, but I can still enjoy it in my mind's eye and imagination.

BRUIJN RASMUSSEN DESIGN

BRUIJN RASMUSSEN MODERNE KUNST

BRUIJN RASMUSSEN TORBEN SØRENSEN'S GLASS-COLLECTION

Ideals of Beauty

MONIR SHAHROUDY   INFINITE POSSIBILITY:
FARMANFARMAIAN   MIRROR WORKS AND DRAWINGS

South American Mythology
THE MAPPING OF THE WORLD

PAGE 20: In a London townhouse, the swirling pattern of Allegra Hicks's fantastic rug, designed for the space, echoes the softened octagonal shape of the room and is bathed in light from the large skylight above. I love sitting in this room with George the scruffy terrier.

PAGES 22–23: I added antiqued mirrored wall panels to balance and reflect the large garden windows opposite and designed radiator covers to look like modern French oak cabinets. A pair of late eighteenth-century architectural capriccios flanks the painting by Massimo Campigli above the mantel.

PAGE 24: The clients have an interesting collection of furniture, paintings, drawings, books, ceramics, and other decorative arts, which I happily mixed throughout the house. A Fornasetti chair, early Georgian stools, a steel desk by John Vesey, and extremely fine carved Empire chairs all get along just fine.

PAGE 25: The cool, open, industrial stair railing contrasts well with the opulence of the gilt-framed Ballets Russes portrait of Nijinsky by Jacques-Émile Blanche.

PAGE 26: In the study of this client, an author and philanthropist, the TV, a happy fact of life, fits perfectly in the bookcase next to the limestone mantel, above which hangs a Toulouse-Lautrec colored lithograph.

PAGE 27: Notable eighteenth-, nineteenth-, and early twentieth-century paintings and works on paper hang above the daybed, on which are strewn tiger-patterned silk velvet, crewelwork embroidery, and pretty, old-fashioned floral-print linen pillows. The cool Italian mid-century floor lamp, designed by Maurizio Tempestini, reflects the husband's ancestry.

PAGES 28–29: In the dining room, Carolina Irving's Patmos printed linen covers the walls. Surrounding the custom burl wood, extending dining table are paisley-covered, French 1940s-style cerused-oak dining chairs. A late eighteenth-century watercolor of the Colosseum hangs above the mantel, and a portrait of the client's dashing father hangs to the right.

PAGE 30: The large tester bed, with hangings made of different fabrics that echo the curtains, stands centered in this octagonal, sunlight-filled bedroom.

PAGE 31: In the dressing room of a favorite client—a pretty and fancy International Best-Dressed Hall of Famer (who could not be any less stuffy)—Brunschwig & Fils' Les Touches printed linen covers the walls in an homage to the fashion designer Geoffrey Beene.

PAGES 32–33: In the living room of this farmhouse in Millbrook, New York, an Indian ceremonial hunt painting of a noble tiger presides over several areas of deep, comfortable seating.

PAGE 34: An open plan of connected rooms allows the clients to entertain easily and effortlessly, which they do often and well.

PAGE 35: The wisteria-entwined pergola is the perfect canopy for this outdoor dining porch, with views of the Catskill Mountains across the Hudson Valley.

PAGES 36–37: As part of the extensive renovation, we worked with Studio Geiger Architecture to add a library (and TV room), which features seating for many, a useful card table, and ample shelves for a superb collection of pre-Columbian ceramics, along with plenty of books, games, and photographs.

PAGE 38: In the Park Avenue apartment of a notable American heiress, the dining room, with its leather chairs à la Nancy Lancaster, Pierre Frey patterned curtains, and beautiful old Chinese Export botanical watercolors on vellum, evokes my love of the chic, classic decorating of David Hicks and Mark Hampton.

PAGE 39: In the library, mahogany bookcases and the woven paisley wall upholstery make the portrait by a Baltic painter and the smart and fun client's extensive collection of books stand out beautifully.

PAGES 40–41: In this living room, multiple seating areas and softly patterned glazed walls create a serene and subtle backdrop for a rich layering of objects and artwork, collected over a lifetime and reflective of the client's family history.

PAGE 42: The banquette sofa, upholstered in moss-green velvet, makes this corner an inviting place to sit and admire the Dutch still life and fine English furniture.

PAGE 43: A pre-Columbian gold mask and English Regency cachepots, painted in imitation of Asian lacquer, sit atop a rare early eighteenth-century japanned chest-on-chest under a Picasso watercolor.

PAGES 44–45: Madeleine Castaing's Branches de Pin printed-cotton fabric upholsters the walls of this Brooklyn family room, while fabrics from Décors Barbares, Carleton V, and Robert Kime work together to represent the client's French, American, and Anglo-Saxon roots.

PAGE 46: A Thonet chaise and Louis XV bergères mingle with a wicker sofa upholstered in Décors Barbares' Sarafane fabric in this light-filled Brooklyn brownstone parlor.

PAGE 47: In the kitchen, the garden is seen through a pair of French doors, bringing the outside in, even on dreary days.

PAGE 48: The client's sister, Nathalie Farman-Farma, designed the Dans la Forêt fabric that covers the Napoleon III tufted chaise, which sits comfortably on the Castaing carpet, amid eighteenth- and nineteenth-century watercolors, a Baltic Karelian birch chest, and an ebonized Thebes stool.

PAGE 49: A bathroom with an old-fashioned claw-foot tub set on the patterned-tile floor is lightened by the pretty Décors Barbares Ete Moscovite café curtains.

PAGE 50: What a great and happy surprise it was to see this shot of the corner banquette in the room I designed for the Kips Bay Decorator Show House on the front page of the *New York Times* Home section!

PAGE 51: The Biedermeier armchair covered in tiger-patterned silk velvet and the leather-and-chrome Danish modern chair by Arne Norell create a sophisticated juxtaposition with the French Deco Macassar ebony desk.

OPPOSITE: The handsome and reserved French neoclassical-style cabinet holds a television and supports a stocked bar tray—two essentials for my dream study.

THE DECORATION OF EVERY HOUSE OR APARTMENT takes its cues from the surrounding environment; houses in the mountains look and feel different from apartments in major cities. Likewise, a house in the tropics requires a different approach from a country house in the Northeast.

As decorators, we have to think logically and carefully when working on projects across the country's varied regions as well as those abroad. We have to consider the materials we use: which ones are going to work and which should be avoided to prevent a potential decorating disaster. If an unnamed, undeniably cute dog enjoys compulsively rolling around and digging in a muddy garden, the furniture and rugs inside need to be reasonably repellent to that mud. There are only so many emergency baths that can be given before said dog jumps all over everything.

My personal predicament aside, I give a lot of thought to the materials that will be appropriate for each job. Chenille fabrics, leather, and suede are fine for houses in colder climates, where the inhabitants aren't going to stick to the upholstery. Fragile straw carpets, however, aren't going to hold up to ski boots stomping heavily across the floor.

And though wicker and straw may be more appropriate at the beach, we should remember that there are no steadfast rules to be strictly enforced by the decorating police. I have an old rattan-and-wicker armchair in my living room in the country, and it is perfectly at home, looks great, and works fine. It is good to be mindful but not rigid.

I laugh whenever I think of what my friend Mary refers to as the Bahamian moose head. I guess a moose head could work on a tropical island if it has a compelling backstory—how it got there, who brought it, and why. But without that backstory, there's an absurdity to overcome. One wouldn't expect to see a giant marlin trophy on the wall of a chalet in the mountains. And I'm not going to suggest saddle barstools or a surfboard coffee table for a suburban house in Indiana. In general, I gravitate toward things that make a bit of sense, and I select and use materials that reflect the specific needs of the specific environments.

The use of stained-oak planks and reclaimed barn wood on ceilings, floors, and walls makes a perfect backdrop for the modern house in the mountains out West, seen on pages 54–63. The upholstered pieces are all covered in durable, soft natural fibers for longevity, and the furniture and accessories are wood, wrought iron, rough ceramics, and stone. There is a moose head (not from the Bahamas) made of balsa wood that lends a bit of humor from its perch overlooking the living room.

A SENSE OF PLACE

I chose very different materials for the hotel I worked on in the island paradise of the Dominican Republic. Tortuga Bay, originally designed by Oscar de la Renta, needed a bit of refreshing. Like a good facelift on a beautiful woman, it had to be a subtle job that didn't startle anyone. We had to make sure the long list of illustrious guests felt right at home when they returned to see the new work. As seen on pages 64–75, we used soft fabrics from de la Renta's collections, straw furniture woven on the island, and mahogany pieces carved locally, all set against the backdrop of the chic coral stone quarried from the island bedrock.

The laid-back vibe of the North Atlantic island of Martha's Vineyard set the tone for the breezily under-decorated house on pages 94–111. Casual furnishings loosely arranged with the family's comfort in mind perfectly suited the house's low-key owners, who didn't even want people to know that they'd hired a New York decorator. Cat's out of the bag now. Anyway, the straw rugs that my family had always had and loved in our house on Lake Michigan look just as cool and easy in this house, where wear and tear only enhance the feeling over time.

Equally easy in a different way is a house in Florida that longtime favorite clients bought and asked me to fiddle with, as it had previously been charmingly decorated. The bedroom on pages 92–93 is for me the epitome of calm and serenity, tailored to the warm climate with crisp white sheets and ivory linen curtains amid the repeated pale-blue Billy Baldwin–designed fabric Arbre de Matisse, which conjures the South of France and gentle breezes. The corner of the loggia on page 91 holds cushioned wicker seating, Indian pottery, and African baskets hung in groups, as well as an un-killable tole agave plant, requiring no care when the snowbirds head back north.

A mountain vacation house for both skiing in winter and fishing, riding, and hiking in summer, seen on pages 76–85, features rough, unfinished pine beams and bleached oak, giving it a light, open, and slightly Scandinavian feel. The furnishings are a mix of mid-century woven-rope-and-wood pieces and contemporary upholstered seating. The dining table is a giant slab of live-edge walnut with casual cushioned benches, which permit flexibility in the number of diners without moving chairs in or out. There's one polished-metal piece—a leather-and-chrome chair by Arne Norell—but it works and is a nod to the Scandinavian heritage of the mistress of the house.

I do love working all over the map, getting to know different parts of the country and the world. Dying to do a ranch in the desert, a villa in Morocco, or a great English country house by Lutyens. Just putting that out there.

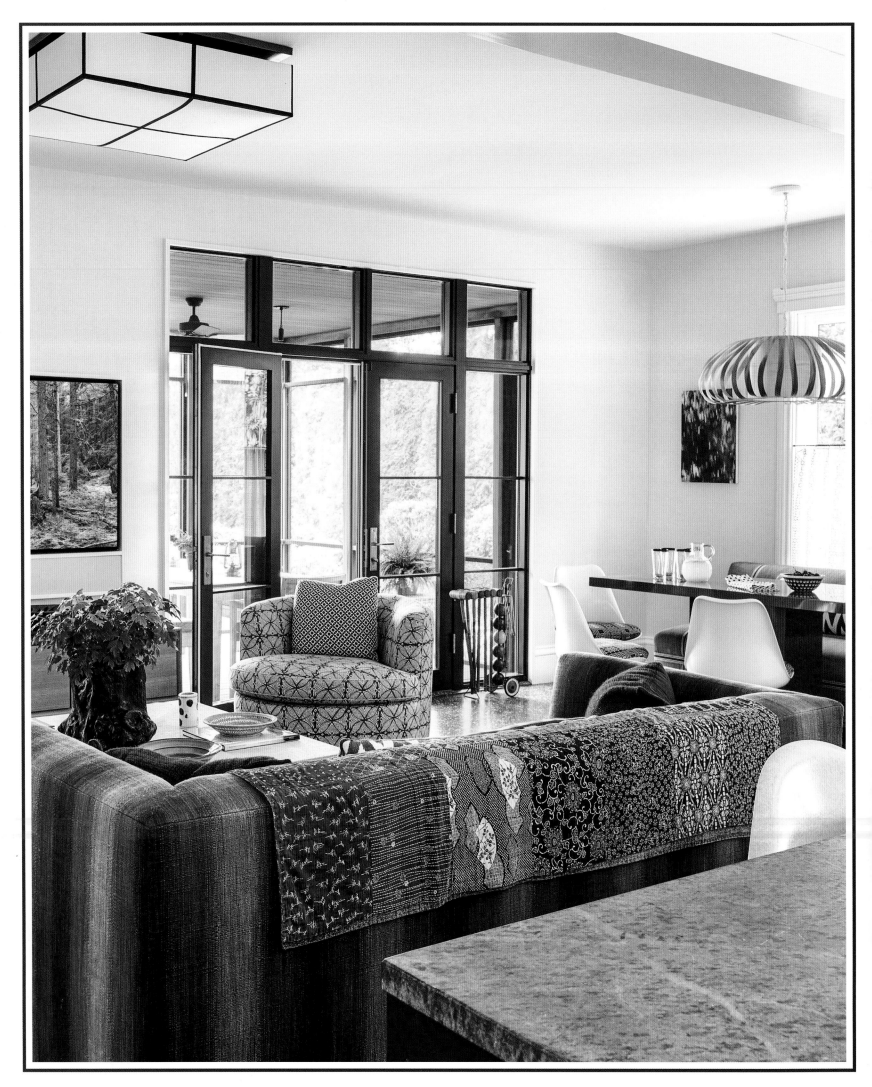

PAGE 54: The entrance hall of this ski house high in the mountains of Montana is clad in reclaimed wood and stone.

PAGE 56: The large photograph by Massimo Vitali hints at what goes on outdoors in winter, while the aspen leaves in the sculpted ceramic vase were found on a late summer hike.

PAGE 57: The balsa wood moose-head sculpture, by Shawn Smith, looks down on the large living room of this slope-side timbered house. It took seven guys to mount it. I hadn't expected balsa wood to be so heavy.

PAGES 58–59: I designed the notched, stained-oak, extending pedestal dining table to center the huge open room.

PAGE 60: A Black Forest sculpture of a stag and a Noguchi paper table lantern attract the attention of the furry bull in the photograph by Alexander von Reiswitz.

PAGE 61: A modernist Bungalow 5 oak desk and a Napoleon III-style upholstered armchair loosen up the mountain references of a Slim Aarons photograph and a Bavarian clock, yet still work harmoniously.

PAGES 62–63: Walls upholstered in moss-colored cashmere and a faux-chinchilla blanket on the paisley-embroidered bed all softly enhance the parchment drum table and Jean-Michel Frank ebonized armchair, but nothing competes with the incredible mountain views.

PAGES 64–65: Coral stone walls, ceiling fans, and slatted shutters keep the heat from rising in this vast clubhouse room of the Punta Cana resort in the Dominican Republic.

PAGES 66–67: Throughout the clubhouse, I used wicker and mahogany, two indigenous Dominican materials. The pressed botanicals by the artist Stuart Thornton were given by Oscar and Annette de la Renta to the resort, which they helped found.

PAGES 68–69: Reception at Tortuga Bay, the resort's chic hotel, originally designed by Oscar de la Renta, which I was hired to refresh in his style, features two tall mahogany bookcases, which he had given to the hotel.

PAGE 70: I designed simple mahogany-and-glass hurricanes to go with the tropical grisaille scenic panel commissioned from decorative artist Elizabeth Hargraves. The pair of nineteenth-century Chinese baluster vases make the room feel more like Oscar.

PAGE 71: Lisa Fine Textile's Luxor fabric covers one of a pair of Oscar-designed sofas. It shares the space with segmented-bone coffee tables and ratcheted-oak plant stands of my design, made locally by Dominican craftsmen.

PAGES 72–73: The coral-red plaster walls of the dining room, trimmed with a de la Renta stripe, and the dining chairs, backed in a de la Renta bamboo-leaf print, give the room its colorful tropical feel. And yes, the palm leaves I arranged on the Serge Roche–inspired center table definitely help.

PAGE 74: The grass-cloth-clad, wicker-filled smoking lounge is the perfect spot to enjoy delicious Dominican rum after dinner. Take it from me.

PAGE 75: The vaulted guest rooms, which overlook the beach, feature Chinese pagoda–shaped bamboo canopy beds, which I had made after a model in Oscar's Dominican house.

PAGES 76-77: Unfinished knotty pine beams and trim work, set against gray-stained oak planking, give this mountain house its Scandinavian appeal.

PAGES 78–79: A Nakashima-inspired dining table, with a live-edge walnut top on a custom base, is flanked by cushioned benches, which offer seating flexibility and lend an informal element to the large, open room.

PAGE 80: The mountain valley, seen from the wall of windows, draws our attention out, so I used luxurious soft fabrics and ultra-comfortable seating to lure our focus back, or at least make us happy while looking at the expansive view.

PAGE 81: The radiating explosion, made of tiny credit-card clippings by artist Robi Walters, is an example of a material choice not necessarily thought of as mountain appropriate but still works in an interesting way.

PAGE 82: I used randomly sized fieldstone blocks from the region for the indestructibly handsome backsplash.

PAGE 83: A basket made from hundreds of glued Popsicle sticks, found at a flea market, serves as a nice pendant over the breakfast table.

PAGE 84: A wood-grained fabric by Carleton V was the perfect solution for a quiet texture on the walls of a guest room. Nice view to wake up to, right?

PAGE 85: With its brown color scheme, the study on the top floor of the house is the perfect place to retreat from needy guests and children.

PAGE 86: In the stair hall of a house in Florida, I kept the existing, tropical-feeling stair railing and added the gessoed Georgian console, the cool artwork, and the wild Ferrick Mason printed linen, which lines the walls above the grass cloth.

PAGE 87: The use of bright and cheery patterns in different greens, along with white-painted beams and woodwork, lights up this large, airy room.

PAGES 88–89: In the living room, I covered the walls in Quadrille's hexagonal Maze linen print as a backdrop for the vibrant artwork.

PAGE 90: An Eve Kaplan chandelier and a photograph by Louise Lawler are the stars of this Palm Beach dining room. Rather than change the existing charming trellis wallpaper, I schemed around it.

PAGE 91: Resin wicker and acrylic fabrics are some of the greatest advancements in decorating, allowing us to furnish outdoor spaces beautifully and to comfortably enjoy rosé and cheese.

PAGES 92–93: Billy Baldwin's Arbre de Matisse printed linen covers the walls and chairs, giving a light and airy feel to this bedroom. The chic mirror by Tilton Fenwick hangs above a painted Jansen commode.

PAGE 94: I did a happy, custom colorway of Schumacher's Hydrangea paper for the walls of this entrance hall on Martha's Vineyard. And I gave the clients' son the Nerf machine gun (after playing with it for a day or two until I forced myself to hand it over).

PAGE 95: A wire chandelier I found for the clients' first apartment many years ago made its way here to hang above the Saarinen table and Swedish dhurrie rug—Finland and Sweden vying for attention in a truly American house.

PAGES 96–97: A rug of straw squares ties together the different areas of the living room, which gets the most use because of the view, the card table, the reading/napping chaise, and the fireplace.

PAGES 98–99: A painting by Olivia Munroe of colorful concentric circles and dots hangs above the mantel. This house is purposefully under-decorated and consequently feels super relaxed.

PAGES 100–101: The big, open family room, breakfast area, and kitchen, designed by Andrew Herdeg of Lake Flato Architects, is a considerable departure from the rest of the shingled, Colonial-style house, but it works perfectly. I especially love the splatter-painted floor I fought for, which I think ties this space to the older architecture.

PAGE 102: I mean, who doesn't want to sit on a porch swing? And, who doesn't appreciate a stocked wicker bar?

PAGE 103: Lisa Fine Textile's Aswan print in green covers the walls of the dining room and reflects the summery greens of the trees and garden outside. Napoleon III gilded faux-bamboo plant stands flank the window and hold baskets with pots of Japanese anemones.

PAGE 104: In the master bedroom, I mixed patterns in muted colors with a jute rug and ivory linen curtains, all so as not to compete with the lovely view outside.

PAGE 105: A handsome Danish desk sits in front of useful trellis-fronted cabinets in the study off the master bedroom.

PAGES 106-7: In the playroom, furry beanbags provide extra seating for a spirited and lengthy Monopoly game, which hopefully gives adults a few hours' respite.

PAGE 108: The Martha's Vineyard–themed pink toile on the bed is enhanced by the unbelievably charming antique American quilt in this guest room.

PAGE 109: Soft pink walls and a Flokati rug are perfect for this sweet girl's room, with its Indian patchwork bedspread and painted spindle bed.

OPPOSITE: The recently added screened porch, overlooking the historic West Chop Lighthouse, is an ideal spot for lunch or dinner without bugs, rain, or the scorching sun.

PRACTICALITY

Yes, because we have to (I'm joking). As boring as it may sound, practicality is key to any successful design. Thinking practically assures clients that you aren't just a silly, trim-peddling pillow fluffer but can address any challenge and come up with effective solutions. And a pretty room is pretty much useless if it doesn't function well. Yes, making beautiful rooms is a goal, but does an attractive room even exist if no one is there to use it? But I digress into metaphysics when the focus of this chapter is on the importance of the applicable.

The design of upholstery, for instance, has to be comfortable and have the right depth, pitch, and softness for its intended use—hall settees are very different from living room sofas or screening room chaises. For all my custom furniture designs—desks with ample storage for printers or files, coffee tables with shelves for family albums and games, or dining tables with a series of leaves for flexible seating—I think about the specific and best use for the piece. And I try to incorporate hides or other materials that won't get ruined with the first brush of human contact.

Practicality can sometimes entail taking the path of least resistance. In our house in the country, I know I am going to have to rip out the existing, weirdly abutting wood paneling and brick chimney breast seen on pages 118–19 when I ultimately redo and add onto the kitchen. I chose to just paint it all white and ignore the awkward design, rather than devise a temporary fix to bridge the gap until I win the lottery and can take on the more daunting addition and kitchen project I am planning.

In the townhouse on pages 112–15, the previous owners had used a decorator whose work I admire. In the living room, the wall covering of bark-paper squares was a material I had used often over the years, so I chose the new furnishings to work with that backdrop. And because I loved the tight animal-print rug and the dark reflective walls in the library on pages 132–33, I suggested we keep them, much to my clients' appreciation, not only because I didn't change elements that were perfectly nice, but also because it saved them money. Given the nature of my job, that isn't something I get to boast about very often.

My favorite cousins found themselves homeless when two properties they owned sold somewhat unexpectedly in rapid succession. We quickly had to assess the contents of a big house in Indiana and a chic apartment in New York, and figure out what would work in a temporary rental house and a new property being built in Montana, seen on pages 124–25. Determining which pieces would go where and how to make them all fit into two completely new and quite different surroundings was like winning a complex game of Rummikub.

I often will hire decorative painters to do faux-wood graining on paneling, walls, ceilings, and/or beams to avoid the cost of having to stain rare or exotic woods. Finding artisans who know how to do beautiful, custom stained finishes, rather than the spray finishes that are prevalent in new construction, isn't easy. At first glance, it may seem impractical to undertake the painstaking job of faux painting, but when compared to the alternative, it is logical, taking less effort and affording greater control over the final result—assuring that the new "paneling" will not look like the interior of a reality TV show mansion.

Kids and pets are a major reality check that forces us to be practical. We need to plan and be prepared for their chaos and mess. I mentioned pets in the previous chapter, but kids and their needs introduce a whole different factor into the decorating equation. Furniture that can be moved around a room to accommodate playtime and case pieces with ample built-in storage are essential. No one wants to be staring at Barbie's pink plastic multiplex dream home during dinner.

Clients' possessions are a reality too. Every once in a while, there's a piece of furniture or a work of art that I have to incorporate into the décor but just can't look at, and I imagine that it bears a little sign reading "This piece was not sanctioned by Markham." Most of the time, however, clients have quite interesting, beautiful things, and we have to think practically about how best to make them fit or work. One client purchased a cool Mediterranean-style house in Texas, seen on pages 136–41, and she came to the project with chic, old-fashioned English and Continental furniture, as well as works of art passed down from her New York family of important collectors. So we carefully managed to work the seemingly uncharacteristic styles of furniture and art for this type of house into a coherent, happy design.

Sometimes, life takes unexpected turns. Recently, I helped a favorite client move from a big, fancy house on Sutton Square to a cool loft downtown so that she would be near her kids and grandchildren. She and her fantastically generous husband were two of my first clients, but he sadly passed away a few years ago. To give her a fresh start, we created a whole new vibe and environment, setting all of her treasured and quite traditional old furniture against the sleek, modern backdrop of the big, open loft seen on pages 146–49. Incidentally, she hates the word *loft* and refers to her new home as a ranch in the sky. She's going to kill me for calling it a loft.

For every project, perhaps the paramount practical consideration is determining how clients are going to use their rooms—and the individual pieces in those rooms. That consideration is uppermost in my mind from the get-go.

PAGE 112: In a New York townhouse on the Upper East Side, the walls are covered with squares of natural bark paper, which I love and have used often. They had been installed by the previous owner's decorator, so I kept them and worked up a new scheme around them.

PAGES 114–15: The clients wanted to be able to seat many guests in this large room yet ensure that they would not feel terribly far from one another. So we employed comfortable sofas and upholstered chairs that could turn toward one group or another. The two large photographs of historic libraries by Massimo Listri confirm the scale of the room.

PAGE 116: This dining table, painted in faux-parchment squares, has the rich look without the fragility and cost of actual parchment. Leaves that expand the table fit within it when not in use. A rare set of late eighteenth-century hand-colored engravings of Sir William Hamilton's collection of geological specimens hangs above the Jansen ebonized cabinet.

PAGE 117: In this dark powder room hall, I covered the walls and bench in the same custom-colored Carleton V Caleb printed linen specifically to highlight the superb Degas ballerina, lit from above.

PAGES 118–19: If you ignore something long enough, it goes away (at least that was my hope for this room). In the entrance hall of our country house, white paint has temporarily made the exposed old brick and random wall paneling less visually prominent and annoying until we renovate. Interesting and varied art, objects, and textiles all help to distract the eye from the mess.

PAGE 120: Every fireplace deserves a comfortable chair next to it, and every chair deserves a footstool, a table to set down a drink or book, and good lighting by which to read. The living room in this Millbrook house is especially cozy in winter. I fell asleep here once when I was supposed to be hanging pictures.

PAGE 121: Clients with four children and numerous friends appreciate synthetic grass-cloth walls, which can withstand peanut-butter-and-jelly fingerprints or suitcase scuffs. Stenciled borders add a little extra visual interest. The well-placed bar is also appreciated.

PAGES 122–23: When you have a giant south-facing bay window and love simple matchstick blinds, you have to think about protecting fabrics from the sun's damaging rays. In the back parlor of our country house, I had the blinds lined with a sheer linen to filter the sun and bound them all around for durability. Harriet is on the lookout for pesky, taunting squirrels.

PAGES 124–25: For a house out west, we used faux-wood-grain wallpaper to help the architecture and the walls feel more substantial and appropriate to the mountain locale. Most of the furnishings used to live in an apartment in New York, but, like Eddie Albert in *Green Acres*, they traded Park Avenue for a life in the country. The addition of pieces such as the Korean mortar-form table and the sculptural African pipes, enhance the less urban, more earthy mode.

PAGES 126–27: The layout and cabinetry of kitchens require a great amount of thought about use and practicality. In this Southampton kitchen, a new addition to a nineteenth-century house, shirred fabric panels behind the glass-fronted cabinets add a bit of warmth and alleviate the pressures of keeping the shelves organized and tidy.

PAGE 128: Donald Judd's plywood boxes inspired the bunk bed I designed for a little boy's room, which gave him not only a cool big bed for himself and one on top for a friend but also bookcases on one end and a ladder on the other, with plenty of extra floor space for Thomas, Percy, and Sir Topham Hatt.

PAGE 129: To save money on costly marble or tile work in our carriage house bathroom in the country, I asked the contractors to use riveted galvanized-metal sheets on the shower walls and poured concrete for the floor. Cheap and cheerful, and quite cool, I think.

PAGES 130–31: In this California house, we needed deep shelves for large books and a collection of Picasso pottery, so I designed floating shelves, which feel lighter and less obtrusive than enclosed bookcases.

PAGE 132: In the library of a townhouse on the Upper East Side, I kept the animal-print rug and chic dark wall treatment, remnants of the handsome design by the previous owner's decorator, Tom Scheerer. Not only were they good looking and easy to work with, but keeping them cost a lot less than ripping them out and starting from scratch. Design inheritance is almost never this accommodating!

PAGE 133: For the dining room, I chose cool Karl Springer Onassis chairs to echo the curved tops of the French doors that overlook the lush garden below.

PAGE 134: I kept the entrance hall of this New York apartment purposefully spare so there would be room for the children's hockey nets. We limited the décor to the large and vivid botanical watercolor by Sarah Graham and an easily movable Karl Springer bench.

PAGE 135: In a New York townhouse, I had the original wooden shutters stripped of thirty layers of crusty old paint so they would function better and decided to leave them unpainted when I saw how good they looked with the tinted and polished plaster walls and the Gino Sarfatti coil chandelier. The painting by Alex Schuchard complements the colorful and varied fabric scheme.

PAGES 136–37: Maybe my favorite image in the whole book is this one of the client's yellow Lab staring intently from the dog-friendly loggia, wanting to come into the slightly less dog-friendly living room in this Texas house.

PAGE 138: A painting by the artist Kayce Hughes hangs above the mantel and helps the fantastic bronzes from the client's family mix with the more modern furnishings.

PAGE 139: Painted eighteenth-century Chippendale candlestands topped by French brass wine coolers holding orchids flank the entrance to the lacquered library in this Mediterranean-style house in Austin.

PAGE 140: The barrel-vaulted dining room features an Italian Baroque dining table, a Qing dynasty altar table that serves as a sideboard, and an English William IV étagère bar cart. It is nice to have clients with interesting things to work with.

PAGE 141: In the library, Pierre Frey's Le Grand Corail fabric on the sofas is contrasted by a tribal-patterned wool rug and chevron-tweed linen curtains; everything looks bright against the dark-chocolate-lacquered walls. The giant Audubon pelican print and the reflective Japanese Wakasa lacquered coffee table offer additional visual and cultural counterpoints.

PAGES 142–43: All synthetic outdoor fabrics, wall coverings, and rugs were used in this modern ski-lodge apartment, where four rowdy brothers and their friends have the run of the place. I suggested to the clients that they move the Japanese Shodai ware vase to a safe place during their residency.

PAGE 144: In this New York library, the deep red of the velvet sofa and matching lacquer walls allows the sitter not to fear spilling red wine. The photograph by Nelson Hancock depicts the dome of the Rumbach Street Synagogue in Budapest.

PAGE 145: Powder rooms are an opportunity to do something pretty and special. I often upholster the walls to absorb sound, as no one wants to hear a toilet flushing during a cocktail or dinner party. For this Greenwich powder room, I used Bennison's China printed linen and converted a Gustavian chest of drawers into the vanity.

PAGES 146–47: Faux leather clads the walls of this big open loft in downtown New York and helps to add a layer of warmth and texture to all of the richly upholstered furniture, which migrated with the client from a stately Sutton Square townhouse to this more casual environment.

OPPOSITE: In the loft's large bedroom, we hung a canopy from the beamed ceiling to create a cozy enclave.

O UR PERSONAL POSSESSIONS, FROM BOOKS TO travel mementos to works of art, all have individual stories to tell. And collectively, they lend depth and character to a room. Much of a room's success comes from incorporating the objects we treasure because they reflect who we are.

A sentimental gift or a childhood toy can elicit fond memories and give pleasure at a mere glance. For me, collected shells and natural specimens spark memories of different beaches or woodland walks with loved ones and remind me of the beauty of the natural world. They also make me think of the importance of conservation and of leaving the world a cleaner and better place.

I'm a bit of a hoarder, as evidenced by the walls of our house in the country on pages 162–65. I am drawn to works on paper and collect a broad range, from old master and nineteenth-century nature studies to contemporary collages. Hanging the art gallery style allows my inner hoarder to shine through. In the living room, there's a Chinese eighteenth-century red-lacquered table with mother-of-pearl inlay that has a beautiful shape and is a work of art in its own right, but it is made much more interesting visually and intellectually by the placement of objects on it and their relationship to each other: an Indian miniature painting, an Austrian glass lamp, a Native American gourd, a Chinese perfume bottle, and a Japanese lacquer bowl. It's like a happy refrain of "We Are the World."

That table keeps company with a mid-century sofa by Arne Norell, an American bamboo-and-rattan armchair, vintage textiles, and a snakeskin coffee table of my own design. Every object in the room plays off of every other, and it is this interplay that I find makes a room vibrant and revealing.

Art and accessories are as important as the wall coverings, window treatments, and furnishings that make up the initial layer of decoration. These finishing touches go the extra step to define the character of any room. My carriage house workspace, seen on pages 4–5 and 188–91, is a big, open, loft-like barn structure clad in pine planking and furnished with colorful upholstery, rugs, and curtains. But it's everything else in there that gives the room its character: the giant lantern (which looks like one of the McDonaldland Fry Guy characters), the big work table I made with an old burled tree trunk as the base, and the old English chest from my bedroom in Boca Grande.

The chic entry hall of a London townhouse on pages 2–3 has a sophisticated, layered scheme. The walls, done in a pale,

LAYERING AND EMBELLISHING

hand-tinted and -dragged plaster to resemble ivory horn, serve as a backdrop to the fine Georgian mantelpiece. The bookcases are backed in nailhead-edged suede and trimmed in faux, segmented dark horn. The furniture ranges from a 1960s steel-and-brass neoclassical desk to early Georgian footstools, finely carved Empire chairs covered in sheepskin, and a single chair by Fornasetti. The African mat and carved-wood drum table lend a casual and bohemian feel to some of the more serious furniture. And the fantastic photograph of snakes energizes the older works of art and the collection of books.

Layering is achieved not only by adding the final accessories but also by mixing colors and patterns. The tranquil blue-and-white bedroom on pages 154–55, for instance, employs a variety of smaller, all-over busy patterns, which work as a whole to soothe the eye and create a more serene environment than small swatches of the fabrics might suggest. I am fascinated by the unexpected ways that patterns work together and by the way our eyes read and see them. The dining room on pages 150–53 is a complete fantasy of romantic color and floral pattern. It is richly appointed with beautiful antiques and china and silver, but the combination of the specific patterns, though all old documents and quite traditional, along with the vibrant colors, give the room a younger and more exciting feel than might be expected from the contents and the Colonial architecture.

Layering can also come from the use of varied materials. The living room on pages 156–57 and 195–97 has highly polished walls to play off the chenille carpet and the rough plaster of the mantel. The room's furnishings are varied: old patinated tole, lacquer, burled wood and brass, gilt bronze, and carved wood that is either painted antique white, cerused, or stained. All of this creates a rich and varied feel, amplified by the gleaming, fractured-resin cubes (each of which weighs more than a baby rhinoceros, and one of which came down on my slow-to-retract finger when I was helping the movers place them) and the worn, carved-raw-oak console.

I should also point out that it's just as important to know when to refrain from adding layers. The ski house TV room on pages 142–43 illustrates the power of restraint and a more judicious use of pattern and accessories. For a family with four boisterous young sons, it made sense to keep the rooms clean and uncluttered.

PAGE 150: The riot of richly layered and colorful patterns in this Greenwich dining room is an homage to the venerated fabric house Braquenié. I employed Papillons Exotiques for the wall upholstery and tablecloth and Coromandel for the camelback settee.

PAGES 152–53: The traditional architecture of this 1930s Colonial Revival American house lends itself to the French fabrics, Persian carpet, Swedish chandelier, Chinese ceramics, and Baltic console.

PAGES 154–55: This serene blue-and-white bedroom in a Manhattan apartment illustrates that the use of multiple patterns can produce an overall calming visual effect. The soft blues of the early nineteenth-century gouache by Camillo de Vito depicting the Bay of Naples add to the effect.

PAGES 156–57: Polished plaster walls, reflective artwork, and light-refracting blue resin cube tables all catch the sunlight pouring into this Upper East Side apartment and highlight the diverse furnishings and custom-designed rug.

PAGE 158: Robin's-egg-blue glazed walls are the perfect backdrop for this lady's study, with charming details such as the Robert Kime linen used for the armchair and curtains, and the chaise, which once belonged to Brooke Astor.

PAGE 159: Softly shirred valances and the serpentine front of the parchment commode have an old-fashioned charm, yet the monochromatic palette and modern chaise give this bedroom a contemporary feel.

PAGES 160–61: Julia Condon's mandala print, hung on the tomato-red cashmere wall upholstery, resonates with the classic patterns of the curtain and sofa fabrics, resulting in a richly decorated sitting room in this Connecticut house.

PAGE 162: In the front parlor of our Second Empire–style house in the country, I hung the works on paper, which James and I collect, gallery style to maximize the number of works my inner hoarder can display and enjoy.

PAGE 163: In the back parlor and entrance hall of our country house, Victorian and Napoleon III chairs, a large Louis XV bergère and ottoman, and an embroidered paisley tablecloth, along with eighteenth-, nineteenth-, and twentieth-century works of art, stretch the limits of what works together in a harmonious design.

PAGES 164–65: One of my favorite possessions is a painting of a beautiful Greek woman, Aliki Diplarakou, by Jacques Favre de Thierrens. My grandfather purchased it from the artist's studio in Paris in the 1950s and hung it in his dressing room. It was given to me many years later by my mother and evokes happy childhood memories on a daily basis. Isn't that what our collected things should do for us?

PAGE 166: Different blue-and-white prints work together to unify this sunny family dining room in Manhattan.

PAGE 167: A large-scale Schumacher blue-and-white floral fabric covers the walls of this country house powder room and completely carries the room.

PAGES 168–69: A custom-colored, geometrically patterned dhurrie rug lends a casual quality to the rather refined and fancy antique furniture in this leafy suburban house living room. French and Italian neoclassical chairs and Asian lacquered coffee tables give the English-style upholstery a cosmopolitan edge.

PAGE 170: An antique, geometrically patterned Anatolian rug is the perfect finishing touch for this stair hall landing of a country house in the Hudson Valley.

PAGE 171: An antique Caucasian runner and a Napoleon III ebonized faux-bamboo armchair add color and texture to the stair hall of our house in the country.

PAGES 172–73: The different patterns of the Carleton V curtain fabric and the custom flat weave rug work with the clients' artwork and the architectural furniture, like the modernist tiered bookcase and the baroque grotto–style carved-wood table base, to give this New York living room panache.

PAGE 174: Soft blue velvet upholstery, ivory linen curtains with Indian-inspired borders, and a soft woven-jute rug combine to make this country bedroom comfortable and pretty.

PAGE 175: In this Manhattan dining room, a Larry Rivers textured painting hangs above an aqua-tinted shagreen cabinet, which relates stylistically to the custom-designed French modernist dining table and chairs. The pink Murano glass lamps and blue chandelier affirm the color palette of the room, established by the custom-colored Décors Barbares fabric on the walls.

PAGE 176: In our bedroom in the country, the deconstructed, muslin-covered, tufted Victorian armchair reminds me of what I do for clients (in making, not ripping apart, upholstery). To illustrate the finished product, I had the slipper chair handsomely covered with an antique paisley to highlight the pattern.

PAGE 177: Nineteenth-century papier-mâché chairs inlaid with mother-of-pearl are among the most ornamental and fragile of furniture designs, not to mention beautiful. But when there is a tufted chaise nearby, no worries, as anyone wanting to sit down will choose the chaise.

PAGES 178–79: Hand-blocked English wallpaper, ivory-and-turquoise-striped silk curtains with purple silk under curtains, Le Manach's Mortefontaine floral chintz, and pom-pom-fringed muslin bed hangings, all come together in a rich and beautifully layered scheme for this Greenwich bedroom.

OPPOSITE: A Charles X verre églomisé mirror frame and silver-and-gray-silk ikat wall upholstery glam up this Park Avenue powder room.

WHENEVER I CAN, I TRY TO DO SOMETHING interesting that surprises my clients or makes them look at things in a different way. Truth be told, there really isn't anything that new about the decorating process. Yes, some decorators have completely unique points of view and strive for a whole new idiom in their work, but I find that my clients appreciate some amount of familiarity, and whether their taste is traditional or modern, they want me to work in that style and not impose anything alien on them. And, whether we're ground-breaking designers or just adept decorators, we're all making curtains and selecting furnishings. So I try when possible to come up with unique ideas that my clients might not expect.

Freely mixing styles is one way to help clients see things differently with ease. In the large living room on the facing page, for instance, I chose the luminous Barovier glass petal chandelier and the Italian glass sconces, both from the 1960s, to play off of the extraordinary eighteenth-century carved and gilded Chinese Chippendale mirror over the mantel. The glass theme extends to the contemporary pink glass low table between the armchairs. Its shape works nicely with the vintage LaVerne metal low table, which has a Chinese scene etched into the top. That table in turn ties into the chinoiserie mirror and resonates with the contemporary bronze drum tables at the ends of the sofas.

These pieces not only look good together but the connections among them also give everything an extra meaning. It can be interesting to carry out those connections in waves and different directions around the room. There are numerous fantastic glass pieces in the room, including the multicolored mirrored box by Roberto Giulio Rida, seen on page 186, but the connections don't have to be (and in fact shouldn't always be) as literal as the use of the same materials. They can come from placement, for example. The French neoclassical library step table in my carriage house studio, seen on page 189, mirrors the staircase on the other side of the banister. One might not expect to see such a fine, handsome piece of furniture in a barn, but the proximity to the staircase helps it work.

Connections can come from contrasts as well. I love the way the completely stripped and functional metal-and-leather armchair interacts with the beautifully carved and ornamented Arts and Crafts cabinet next to it on page 188. Opposites attract. Similar characteristics work too. I enjoy seeing the ombré stripe on a glazed lamp that I commissioned

SOMETHING DIFFERENT OR UNEXPECTED

from Christopher Spitzmiller next to the stripes on the curtain panels.

Those curtains are a good example of trying something different. I was inspired by the way the red striped embroidery on Ukrainian folk blouses looks against simple white cotton. Wanting the curtains in this giant, pine-paneled space to be bright and whimsical, I collected a wide variety of trims and strips of patterned fabrics and crewelwork, all as potential candidates to consider for the curtains. Suddenly it dawned on me that I didn't have to choose among them but could use them all. When I took the pile of about thirty scraps of trim and all the different fabrics to my curtain workroom, I was afraid they might throw me out, but as always, the team at Anthony Lawrence Belfair was game and open minded and helped me get exactly what I wanted.

Whether I am trying something quite subtle, like the tiny, hand-painted, seismograph-like stripes on the stained-wood floor in the hall on page 193, which are meant to echo the larger, randomly spaced stripes in the Moroccan pile rug, or I'm devising grander gestures like the large, floor-to-ceiling, suede-upholstered, nailhead-edged doors with the amorphously shaped, Giacometti-esque, rough nickel doorknobs I had commissioned, seen on page 192, it can all work together, even if subliminally, to give the room a special feeling or quality.

I once proposed two different ideas for a powder room to a client with whom I had just begun working. One was to cover the walls with mirrored panels custom-etched in a trellis pattern with intertwining vines, a concept I had come up with in some not-terribly-realistic, fevered decorator reverie. The other was a more financially palatable scheme to do a beautiful lacquer job. I meekly showed her the lacquer idea but jokingly told her I had thought of something else that would probably force her to take out a mortgage.

She laughed and replied, "Honey, I didn't hire you because I wanted to save money! I want to see your very best ideas." She told me to figure out the design and the cost and get right back to her, and we ended up doing it. I was so pleasantly surprised by her reaction and her willingness to do something completely lavish and made just for her. That dream client opened my eyes early on in my career, and since that meeting, when pitching ideas I will sometimes propose two different schemes, one with the alternate cost approach. Clients often decide to go with the more extravagant concept, but they always appreciate my having thought to give them the option.

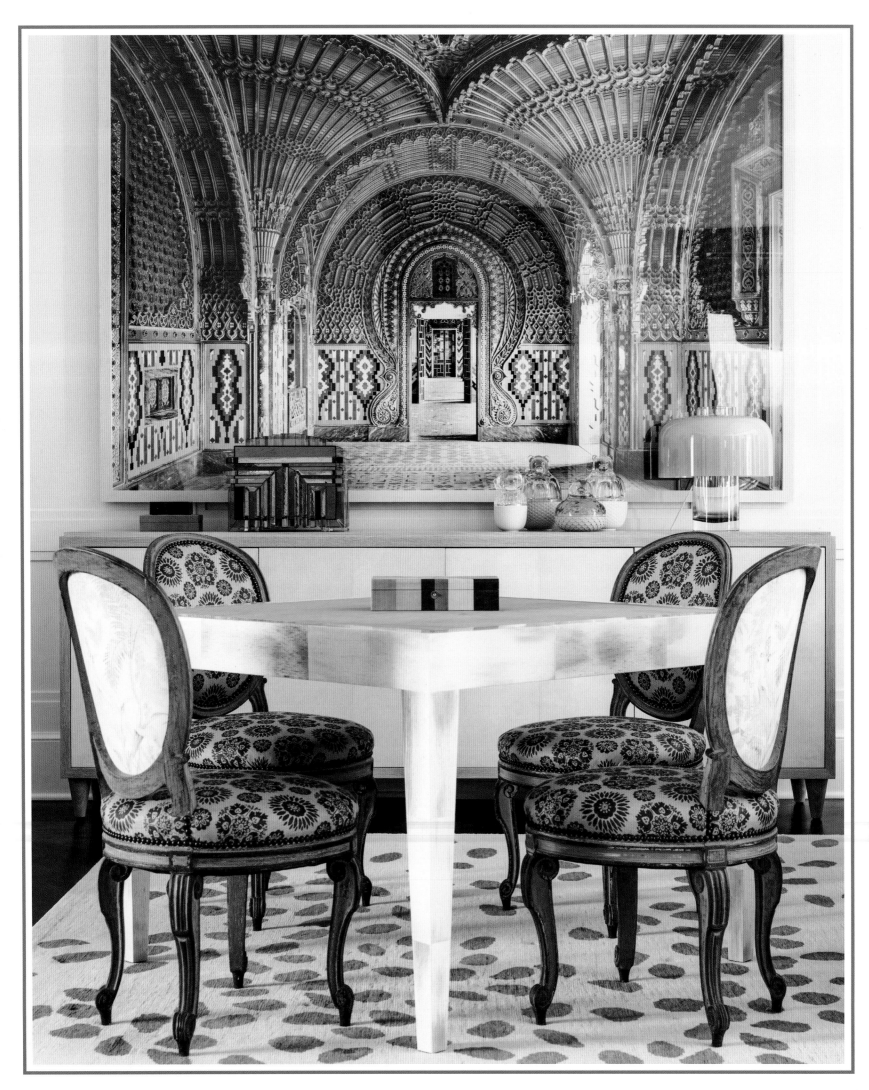

AROUND THE WORLD IN 125 YEARS
EUROPE & AFRICA

AROUND THE WORLD IN 125 YEARS
THE AMERICAS & ANTARCTICA

AROUND THE WORLD IN 125 YEARS
ASIA & OCEANIA

PAGE 182: The finely carved and gilded Chinese Chippendale mirror works beautifully with the more modern Barovier petal chandelier and Italian glass sconces in this house in Beverly Hills, making the leap from the 1760s to the 1960s.

PAGES 184–85: Jewel-toned fabrics against pristine white-painted paneling and gray marble trim make a great backdrop for the varied furniture groupings and artwork, all grounded by the custom turquoise-and-ivory terrazzo-inspired rug design.

PAGE 186: Late eighteenth-century painted Louis XVI chairs, designed by Georges Jacob, surround the segmented faux-ivory card table, which I designed to work with the large Massimo Listri photograph of the Moorish-inspired Palazzo Sammezzano in Tuscany.

PAGE 187: In the series of wide, sunlit hallways, custom inlaid floral medallions of bleached woods enhance and elevate the stained-wood floor.

PAGES 188–89: In my carriage house studio in the country, a Milo Baughman swivel chair, a late eighteenth-century French neoclassical metamorphic library step table, an industrial metal-and-sheepskin armchair, a fine Arts and Crafts cabinet, a lacquered Rietveld Zig-Zag chair, and a Thonet end table all make me very happy.

PAGES 190–91: Rough, unfinished pine planks were the cheapest wood paneling material I could find to finish the restored space between the timbered beams, but they happily smell delicious and remind me of the finer paneling in my family's cottage on Lake Michigan when I was growing up. Harriet enjoys a (rare for her) quiet moment on the Swedish flat weave rug.

PAGE 192: In the entrance hall of a Manhattan apartment, upholstered, nailhead-edged, floor-to-ceiling doors and an important Italian Empire parcel-gilt armchair hold their own with the Lucian Freud study of a horse.

PAGE 193: The dining room's Jupe table and custom Lucite-beaded lantern are seen beyond the cashmere-and-wool-upholstered walls of the entrance hall.

PAGE 194: I designed a pair of demilune commodes with felt-lined drawers to hold the client's silverware. Patterned borders on the silk-burlap walls create the effect of paneling and also line up with and match the curtain trim.

PAGE 195: I had this grotto-like plaster mantelpiece made to work with the Warhol portrait above—crazy sculpting to complement his crazy hair.

PAGES 196–97: A segmented banquette sofa sits between Dupré-Lafon end tables, under a Damien Hirst triptych, and behind equally bright and brilliant fractured-resin cube tables.

PAGE 198: A custom woodland mural by Anne Harris is the backdrop for an Anglo-Chinese console, Palissy ware vase, and Federal convex mirror.

PAGE 199: The entry hall of this American Colonial-style house in Greenwich has a German Biedermeier commode, a Swedish Gustavian clock, and an English Wedgwood agateware urn.

PAGES 200–201: Matchstick blinds shield the living room from the harsh rays of the sun. Pieces of disparate styles, including a George III console, a Karl Springer bench, and an African drum table blend harmoniously. We covered the walls in a bright white plaster and kept the layout relatively spare to give an almost loft-like quality to this Park Avenue apartment.

PAGE 202: An Alex Schuchard painting interacts beautifully with a Charles X specimen marble–topped side table and a nineteenth-century Korean lacquer low table.

PAGE 203: Owing to its size, the banquette, upholstered in bronze-green cotton velvet, had to be made in the room. It is offset by Julia Condon's colorful mandala prints, which echo the round French leather-topped low table from the 1940s.

PAGES 204–5: Tweed-upholstered walls, a parchment-and-oak sideboard, and a giant Art Deco light fixture complete the serene, tailored look of the breakfast room in this California house with its Swedish flat weave rug and upholstered English chairs.

PAGE 206: Naively painted marbleized floors contrast with the white-painted wood paneling in this Southampton bathroom.

PAGE 207: The beamed and paneled ceiling of this summery Southampton bedroom is painted to resemble bleached wood, highlighting the plaster chandelier.

PAGES 208–9: The walls in this large media room are covered with panels upholstered in Carolina Irving's Fuji print, which absorb sound and allow the clients to rotate their art collection, including this Richard Misrach photograph of a surfer.

PAGE 210: Vintage and contemporary pieces such as the floor lamp by Pierre Guariche and the spiky bronze planter by Mike Livingston lend depth and character to the room.

PAGE 211: A large console table that I made out of a giant slab of wood I found, supported by trunk-form bases, anchors one side of the large room.

PAGE 212: An Ellsworth Kelly hangs in an airy Southampton dining room with ivory-lacquered walls, an Italian coral chandelier, and custom, shell-encrusted hurricanes made by Eduardo Garza.

PAGE 213: A photograph from Clifford Ross's *Waves* series hangs on painted battened paneling and above a tufted banquette and custom oak table in a Southampton kitchen with painted floors.

PAGES 214–15: To achieve this beautifully paneled library, we clad the walls in new wood paneling, which we had carefully painted with a subtle wood-grain finish in the perfect warm tone of amber-colored oak.

PAGE 216: The oak-and-parchment cabinet opens to reveal a custom bar, fitted with glasses, cocktail paraphernalia, and liquor bottles, all locked away in preparation for the kids' upcoming teenage years.

PAGE 217: I faded and quilted the Le Manach Batik Raisin fabric for the comfortable armchair and quilted the bronze-green wool felt for the Jean-Michel Frank–style sofa, which sits beneath a painting by Wayne Thiebaud.

PAGE 218: My client inherited Toulouse-Lautrec's painting of Boulou, the artist's Chihuahua, which we hung in the powder room over an English Regency neo-Egyptian pedestal table, all set off by Braquenié's Mauresque Rayure fabric.

PAGE 219: Cork lines the ceiling of this blue-lacquered bar, and the floor is painted like figured burl wood to balance the effect.

PAGES 220–21: This upholstered and paneled screening room in Los Angeles is the perfect place to watch *King Kong*.

PAGE 222: The nickel-trimmed shelving and geometrically patterned ceiling augment this glamorous masculine library in a Hollywood house.

PAGE 223: In this dining room, the rock crystal chandelier hangs over a custom-designed pedestal dining table with Macassar ebony chairs and a chic Art Deco commode by Maurice Dufrêne.

OPPOSITE: For this corner of a living room, anchored by a Robert Delaunay Eiffel Tower painting, I upholstered an antique neoclassical carved and painted settee in strips of different colorways of the same printed linen, separated by rows of gimp trim.

WHEN THE FATES ALIGN, SOMETHING EXTRAOR-dinary can happen.

A client came to me one freezing January day and asked me to work on a house that was being built on the island of Nantucket—a fantastic place to visit in mid-summer, but not super easy to get to in the depths of winter. The client was not satisfied with the architectural design of the house, and, given the fact that construction was already well underway and that the island had strict rules about what could and could not be done, there was an urgency to get the architecture in order. Any changes to the house's footprint or even the window placements would have to be submitted for time-consuming review. Everything told me not to take on this project, that it would probably just be a big hassle.

Fortunately, the client's charm outweighed my initial skepticism. She is smart, funny, naughty, and consequently, great company. She could also be demanding, as she was very much accustomed to a certain way of life, but she has a great sense of irony and could laugh at herself disarmingly.

Early on, I got an email from her instructing me to change the way my office computer system printed things so that they would be easier for her to read, which would have required an entire revamping of our computer coding. To explain that to her, I sent her an email with the subject line: "and the award for the most ridiculous and spoiled client request goes to . . ." She called me immediately, laughing, and I knew we would have not only a great working relationship but a true friendship as well.

We were able to quickly and substantially improve the proposed rabbit warren arrangement of the master and guest-suite baths and dressing rooms without altering the window placement and to work out the complicated plan of different paneling treatments, trim, and built-in cabinetry throughout. Once all that was accomplished, we set about decorating. This client had read my first book cover to cover, and she knew and respected my work. I could tell that she trusted me to come up with something special for her.

When a client gives you free rein to design everything from custom quilts for the beds to pillows made of a dozen different fabrics sewn together in a patchwork pattern, you know you're dealing with someone with a keen interest in decorating and the will and means to let you create something unique. She completely indulged my creativity on every level. She had previously decorated many houses with a wonderful decorator who had retired, so she knew all about high-end custom work. Having worked with great artisans over the years, she wanted to continue to support them. Consequently, we got to create fantastic painted floors with the great decorative painter Bob Christian. We made beautiful woven rugs with Hillary Anapol

THE FATES

of Nantucket Weaver, hand-loomed in the island's traditional method. And we worked with John Danzer of Munder-Skiles on all the outdoor teak furniture designs.

I was able to involve my workrooms in the project and challenge them in new ways, most notably with the difficult job of the wall upholstery for the dining room, creating a pattern of paneling from the direction of the ticking stripe. It was extremely precise work to align every seam perfectly, and the team at Anthony Lawrence Belfair realized my design beautifully. An extremely subtle treatment, it is unpretentious and fitting for a house on a windswept island, as well as a quiet nod to the client's great sophistication.

The short time frame aside, the real challenge of the job proved to be in culling and highlighting the client's extensive collections and possessions. There were at least three different warehouses of catalogued furniture and artworks, collected over a lifetime. I admired many items immediately and came to appreciate others. We devised inventive ways to display things so that the house didn't look like an overrun curiosity shop and cause the person charged with dusting to quit in tears. For example, the already occupied end tables didn't have room for the client's important collection of carved and painted wooden birds, so I split the flock and mounted them on wall brackets in two different areas, employing the groupings as sculptural art for the walls. This job was deftly handled by Dan Sellars, an expert art installer, who also made two complete sets of antique Nantucket stacking baskets appear to float magically, high up on the walls of the entrance hall.

It was a challenge to come up with storage solutions for all the client's impedimenta. I had to think about summer and winter and every possible use of the house by the client alone and by her larger family. But mostly it was a thrill to play with floral and geometric patterns and figure out how they could interact and work off each other in a way appropriate for a summer house on an island. Though the decorating was neither casual nor easy, it needed to look it.

Something made this client buy my book and decide to hire me instead of anyone else. And something made me take this job when I thought I probably shouldn't bother. I had absolutely no idea just how great it would ultimately be to work on this specific house with someone so interesting and generous and fun. There were lots of hurdles to get over and issues to solve along the way, but every challenge had a gratifying outcome. All sorts of artisans and craftsmen came together to make the house come alive, and what a wonderful experience it was for all of us. Whether it was pure chance or the fates looking over us, I don't care. I'm just happy and thankful it happened.

PAGE 226: When a client has all sorts of extraordinarily beautiful things, like lovely plates, glasses, and silver for the table, as well as antique majolica shells and Chinese Export ceramics to hold plants, it makes my job that much easier.

PAGE 228: Two complete sets of antique Nantucket stacking baskets were hung as sculptural elements high up on the entrance hall walls.

PAGE 229: In the entrance hall, Dutch and Chinese blue-and-white ceramics and a pair of old tole topiary trees from the auction of Bunny Mellon's estate welcome guests. And the set of eighteenth-century Indian watercolors of birds of prey lets the visitors know they're being watched.

PAGES 230–31: In the expansive upper hall, an antique quilt, old Palissy ware baskets of fish, large watercolors of great blue herons by Scott Kelley, and mirrors framed with ceramic wave forms and gull heads by sculptor Gail Dooley all give a nod to the surrounding landscape.

PAGE 232: We made a new mantelpiece based on an early American model, then painted and washed it for age and charm. Tole scabiosa flowers by Carmen Almon adorn the mantel, along with an old captain's telescope and scrimshaw objects.

PAGE 233: In the living room, artist Bob Christian created the fanciful tree-of-life mural, inspired by all the fabrics in the room. The mural panels separate and slide behind the flanking bookcases to reveal the big flat-screen TV, which everyone loves having in the room but doesn't want to see when not in use.

PAGE 234: The slipcover, old textiles, and array of pillows on the deep, comfortable sofa soften the fine mirrored and gilded Georgian brackets and the superb Chaekkori scholar's painting hanging above.

PAGE 235: An incredibly intact tramp art table, made of slices of twigs arranged in patterned rows, holds a collection of interesting objects and a cool modern terra-cotta lamp.

PAGES 236–37: In the dining room, the floor, painted in a trellis pattern with floral medallions, and the summery, floral-patterned linen slipcovers balance the more rigid "architecture" of the wall upholstery. The early nineteenth-century English framed shellwork floral still life (one of a pair) and the pair of colossal Minton majolica nautilus-shell planters on plinths strike distinctly fancy notes.

PAGE 238: The powder room walls are upholstered in the same blue-striped fabric and red trim that the client and I had admired in a room designed by Katie Ridder, so I wanted to hang the Palissy ware plates and platters of crustaceans and fish all over to make it feel different. I told Katie that I was ordered to copy it, hoping she would be flattered, rather than annoyed.

PAGE 239: With its ultra-comfortable seating, the family room has a soothing color scheme of soft blues and whites in varying floral and geometric patterns. Even on a rainy day (or during a hurricane, as on the day we photographed), the view of the marshes is incredible.

PAGES 240–41: Breakfast is a treat in this house. Delicious croissants and fruit, iced coffee and fresh-squeezed juice, eggs and crisp bacon are served beautifully on an old marble-topped baker's table. The kitchen windows look out on the extensive flower garden.

PAGE 242: The Bamboo Guest Room takes the theme seriously and employs a riot of beautiful, colorful patterned fabrics. The curtains are Décors Barbares' Ete Moscovite, which inspired the whole scheme.

PAGE 243: In the adjoining bathroom, I grouped the client's collection of antique carved shore birds together and had them mounted as a flock on stands above the tub.

PAGES 244–45: In this guest room, the curtain rods, desk, chairs, bed, and nightstands further the bamboo motif, but what I love most about the room is the mixture of fabrics, especially the intricate quilt that I had made for the bed.

PAGE 246: In the granddaughter's room, sailor's valentines and painted wheelback side chairs stand out against the pale columnar stripes of floral vines painted by Bob Christian.

PAGE 247: The American four-poster bed with simple eyelet hangings is a little girl's dream, where she can snuggle with her stuffed animals and look out over the beautiful water views.

PAGES 248–49: In another guest room, an old Welsh carved-and-limed-wood chest, antique Indian quilts, and custom Leontine linens on the bed are perfect accompaniments to Lee Jofa's sublime Althea floral linen print, which upholsters the walls and a chair.

PAGE 250: For the client's morning room, I asked Bob Christian to paint the walls in faux driftwood graining and made Bohemian curtains of unlined Indian printed cotton from Les Indiennes, all to tone down the fanciness of the famous needlepoint rug designed by Billy Baldwin for the dining room in Bunny Mellon's New York townhouse.

PAGE 251: The Meret Oppenheim ostrich-foot table tempers the snootiness of the antiques in this room, including the Regency painted settee and Georgian gessoed mirror.

PAGE 252: In the bedroom of the lady of the house, Bennison's Chinese Paper linen covers the walls and is used for the curtains. The bed hangings are ivory linen and Pierre Frey's Plumettes cotton print. In combination, they create a calm yet enveloping feeling.

PAGE 253: The geometrically patterned painted floor and the fabric-covered ceiling give this white-painted, wood-paneled bathroom a warmer charm.

PAGES 254–55: The house has two master suites for different family members. This rather masculine and restrained one, for the client's son and daughter-in-law, has a sweeping view of the ocean and a bird sanctuary tidal marsh.

OPPOSITE: The eighteenth-century provincial Italian painted and rush-seated settee came from the estate of Dominick Dunne. It sits beneath three of Julia Condon's set of seven round mandala paintings. Depicting the chakras of the body, they are hung here and at the other end of the entrance hall.

THE EVOLUTION OF A HOUSE

THERE IS NOTHING NICER THAN THE COZY FEELING we get from an old friend, and houses can be like the best of old friends in the joy they give us, the memories they hold, and the familiarity and comfort they provide.

James and I are lucky to have a cottage in the Pacific Northwest, where we can never spend enough time. It's a place we long to get to and dread having to leave. It's sort of an odd little house, full of quirks and charm, but it means so much to us in different ways. For James, it is steeped in history and family memories. For me, it is equated with vacation (and no phone calls or emails or decisions or questions). And for our pup, Harriet, it means the freedom to run up and down the beach and retrieve countless sticks. We all agree, however, that it's the most beautiful and relaxing spot on earth for us.

The house, an old sea captain's cottage on a cliff overlooking the shipping lanes of Puget Sound, had belonged to James's parents, and he spent summers there as a child. Later, when circumstances in life brought the house back into his family, we were presented with an opportunity to redo it, especially because it had been neglected for a long period. But it took quite a few years before the house finally became James's and mine alone, and with that security we were able to really go at it and make it entirely our own. The house is now truly reflective of us and of our interests. And it is a perfect demonstration of how a house can evolve over time, getting better and better the more thought and effort put into it.

The very first thing we did when we initially got the house years ago was to strip the awful mauve and burgundy fake-Victorian wallpapers and borders, cherished by a former tenant, from the walls and paint everything a cleansing white (we torched some sage, too, to exorcise any demons of bad taste). The house worked fine like this for many years, when different members of the family shared it, but once it became solely ours, we got to do everything we had dreamed of doing. Covering the walls with the fabrics and papers we loved was probably the most gratifying to me. I had come up with a custom colorway of my friend Nathalie Farman-Farma's great Décors Barbares print Casse-noisette especially for the dining room but had held the fabric in storage for ages, waiting to do a bit of renovating before putting it up. Now it seems like it has been there forever.

The walls of our bedrooms and dressing rooms upstairs are now covered in the perfect Morris and Godwin papers and fabrics. I had imagined them so many times in my mind's eye, but nothing compared to finally seeing them installed. They make such a handsome backdrop to all our things and add a strong layer of depth and visual interest.

No longer having to worry about anyone else's dogs shedding or messy children eating dripping chocolate Popsicles, we could use our collection of vintage textiles with abandon on pillows and the upholstered seating. We've commissioned and collected art for the house over the years, and with every addition, the overall result is better. A textural Palissy ware plate depicting sea creatures on a mossy water bed, seen on page 22, looks fantastic beneath a late eighteenth-century watercolor of a sea gull, and they both play off of a contemporary painting of a garden by our friend the artist Anthony Prud'homme. Each and every addition to the house interacts with everything previously there, and the decoration evolves and improves.

The most recent and probably the biggest change was our renovation of the old carriage house, which now comfortably (and separately) holds guests. It was in terrible shape, mostly just used for storage, until we gutted it, opened up windows, and paneled the walls and ceilings in warm knotty pine. Guests now have their own spacious domain with views of the water and the back garden, which we've begun working on. And I have a space to sketch, draw, and design in front of a big picture window that overlooks the sea and the snow-capped volcano across Puget Sound.

I remember the first night I ever spent in the house almost twenty years ago, when James and his sisters first got the house back. The rooms were almost empty, except for a bed delivered from the mattress store and two Adirondack chairs from the hardware store in town. Now, with passing time and all of our accumulated stuff, it risks looking a little like Fred Sanford's house, but it's ours and we love it. We added things slowly over the years, and every last piece brings to mind a specific memory, whether happy or sad, but that is life. When a friend who had frequently hosted us at his weekend house in Connecticut passed away, we purchased much of the furniture from a sale of his possessions and had it all shipped out to this house. One of the paintings hanging above the mantel in the living room, seen on page 270, is an oil sketch of our friend's living room, showing the old slipcovered sofa and wicker chairs and tables that now sit happily in our rooms. That little painting is a window on the past, and is but one of hundreds of happy associations we get from our collected treasures filling this house.

PAGE 258: In our Port Townsend house, glossy painted floors and crisp white woodwork set off the patterns of colorful Bessarabian kilims and artwork.

PAGE 260: We usually have drinks on the sun porch before dinner. The 1930s blue pitcher and glasses painted with sailboats seem appropriate to the setting. The large Native American straw basket holds minerals collected from the Grand Canyon.

PAGE 261: With its tall windows providing abundant light and its southern, eastern, and western exposures, the sun porch makes an excellent greenhouse for the plants we foster during our summer occupancy.

PAGE 262: It is lovely to watch the light fade over the water and mountains beyond as we play backgammon. The painted-wicker chaise at the end of the porch makes an ideal reading (mostly napping) spot.

PAGE 263: Harrie enjoys the fine art of relaxing on the big sofa, which our first dog, Choppy, would choose when it was in its former location, the country house of a favorite friend who passed away. For years we spent some of our happiest, funniest weekends in that house on that sofa, and it is still slipcovered in the same old-fashioned chintz, Brunschwig & Fils' La Portugaise, as it was then.

PAGES 264–65: Fabrics, old textiles, and rugs that don't match exactly coloristically can nevertheless work beautifully together to make an interesting scheme for a big room with a lot of seating. The red, white, and blue palette is slightly more exotic, yet still distinctly American.

PAGE 266: My movie seat (no cable TV in this house—just movies or downloaded shows) makes me feel like a patient in a fancy old Swiss sanitarium, where I plan to retire. Julia Condon's mandala prints and Karen Connell's fireworks photograph hang above a table covered with old American falling block–patterned quilt.

PAGE 267: The two-faced fish vase, out of which I made this lamp, was found at JF Chen in Los Angeles, and I knew I wanted it for this spot. I assembled four of artist Anthony Prud'homme's color-study squares into quadrants and framed them. Sharing the tabletop are an old colored-glass electrical conductor and small glass sea urchins I found at the local farm and crafts market.

PAGE 268: The scurrying crab, carved from a moose antler and looking a lot like the crabs on the beach below, turns away from the magnifying-lens bowl holding locally procured seashells and lucky beach glass.

PAGE 269: An old Japanese carved-wood hibachi makes an excellent container for the big spray of hydrangeas and cut greenery from the cliff-side garden. The handsome wicker rocker, another piece that had belonged to our old friend, is super sturdy and comfortable, and you can really get going while having a drink and watching the last rays of the setting sun light up the snow-capped volcano, Mount Baker.

PAGE 270: An American pilgrim chair, with its turned and chip-carved decoration, is an interesting counterpoint to the Ashanti stool, the form of which is one of my favorite designs. It derives from early Egyptian pillows, which I first learned about as a child, when my mother was a docent at the Indianapolis Museum of Art.

PAGE 271: An eye portrait in the Victorian tradition, painted on an oyster shell by Lauren Cherry, rests on a collection of crystal deities and mineral specimens, providing good energy to appease the volcano across Puget Sound and keep it dormant, unlike Vesuvius, pictured in the naïve nineteenth-century gouache of the Bay of Naples.

PAGE 272: In the dining room, the charming, classical American chest holds linens, silver, and candles, and makes the sea otter statue, found in an antiques store in town, feel safe and protected.

PAGE 273: An old portrait of our first dog, Choppy the wild poodle, rests in front of the big vitrine cabinet, which holds natural specimens collected on the beaches of Port Townsend and Boca Grande and on our travels elsewhere, mixed with those collected by James's family over the years.

PAGE 274: An old batik tablecloth covers the white-painted Eastlake dining table, set with Aesthetic Movement plates and Art Deco Lucite flatware. The mirror beautifully reflects the light from the window overlooking the back garden.

PAGE 275: The faux-bamboo, marble-topped serving table fits the period of the house perfectly, in contrast to the spare, geometric, contemporary architectural study of light falling in a room that hangs above it. A little framed print of a shell by Odilon Redon shares the table with a majolica oyster-form compote.

PAGE 276: Mirror, mirror on the wall, who's the best decorator of them all?

PAGE 277: The waterside guest room, with walls covered in the famous Colefax and Fowler Bowood paper, is an old WASP-y, hippie boho hodgepodge. I love the cheap, fragile paper parasol lantern that I had made (can't believe it survived the shipment intact!) and the beautiful muslin curtains, which block the glaring morning sunlight from guests' eyes.

PAGE 278: We've kept the old soft-pink-painted wicker desk, in case someone ever wants to write a note at some point, though phones have pretty much eliminated that need.

PAGE 279: The quirks of this old cottage, like the raised threshold to the stairs and living room beyond, are the very reasons I am drawn to it. Nothing is perfect and certainly needn't be. The goal is to relax and let go.

PAGES 280–81: Harriet loves the old chaise in our bedroom, with its prime view of the cliff and the water below. The chaise isn't very comfortable, but it's fine, and the thought of replacing it seems extravagant and a hassle. I am my grandmother.

PAGE 282: The big Victorian hulk of a chest was James's first purchase at auction as a teenager. On the walls is one of my favorite fabric designs, E. W. Godwin's Bamboo, which reminds me of pot leaves and lulls me peacefully to sleep.

PAGE 283: James's childhood bed, which had been his grandfather's and others' before him, now resides in my dressing room. It makes a nice place to read or to lay out a suitcase when packing. Lots of pattern in this room, and it all works to make me happy.

PAGE 284: Fashion photographer Doug Inglish's photograph of a handsome model sitting on top of the Georgian chest reminds me to get out and exercise.

PAGE 285: An old American desk from James's family holds my papers, as well as sweaters and extra toiletries. With a lack of space in the bathroom, we make do. The photograph, after Hiroshi Sugimoto, is of Bainbridge Island through the mist from the ferry the first time I crossed the Sound with James on our way to the house.

PAGES 286–87: We broke through the wall that had long covered up the old carriage house doors to make this big picture window overlooking the water. It's the perfect spot for my very basic desk—from the purchase of which I learned that Ikea doesn't deliver or assemble. I still love it and the task lamp too.

PAGE 288: Wicker and old upholstery make this room a nice spot for guests to relax. There's a kitchenette/bar behind the portiere. Cladding the walls with raw pine planks proved to be a good solution; everything looks great against them, from textiles stretched as canvases to old Catesby bird prints.

PAGE 289: The sea eagles rule the room from their perch, just as the bald eagles do outside. They seem disinterested in Harrie, but we aren't taking any chances. The small, square painting of a beautiful road nearby is by Anthony Prud'homme. A nineteenth-century paisley textile hangs in the corner above the skirted table.

PAGES 290–91: We've transformed the former hayloft of the carriage house into a nice big guest room. It has views of both the Sound and Chetzemoka Park, with its ancient trees. Okay, I do sometimes hum the Three's Company theme when I'm up there—just needs a spider plant.

OPPOSITE: Guests need nice sheets, a place to put their water and their book or phone, a good reading light, and a soft landing for their feet; with that and a TV, they should be perfectly comfortable and happy.

I dedicate this book to my mother, Juliet Cain Roberts, who rebelled a bit against the quite formal, very proper but beautiful style of her upbringing, and taught me the fun in going out on a limb a little. She would always arrange furniture perfectly without a second thought, and she loved to mix colors and patterns in exuberant ways. Our house in the 1970s was a mix of handsome Georgian furniture that my parents had inherited, modern steel, brass, and glass tables, and vibrant contemporary art that gave the rooms extra punch. My mother is full of solid advice, but she never pushes it on anyone. She taught me so many things I appreciate, like having one table in a room with lots of photographs, rather than trying to "vanity decorate" with framed pictures everywhere. On a broader level, she showed me that things of personal interest, charm, and wit can fill rooms with personality and make all the difference. She also taught me one of my favorite words and just how to say it: Hideous!

ACKNOWLEDGMENTS

FIRST AND FOREMOST, I MUST THANK MARK AND NINA Magowan, along with Beatrice Vincenzini, for allowing me and encouraging me to do a second book. Working with everyone at Vendome was even better the second time around. I am grateful again to the brilliant editor Jackie Decter for her expert handling of my text, and to designer Celia Fuller for her artistic eye and great ideas.

I thank Nelson Hancock for his beautiful pictures, superb photographic skills, and extra efforts all along, and especially for not having succumbed to either the swamps or the snowdrifts— or the even more dangerous car hummus, for that matter. It was a great pleasure getting to work with Bjorn Wallander, Thomas Loof, Miguel Flores-Vianna, Leonora Hamill, and Stephen Kent Johnson. I love how they each captured my rooms.

Biggest thanks to my friend Alison Levasseur, who has championed my work all along and made me feel great, but I am especially proud now to have her lovely foreword. Perhaps the sharpest and clearest eye belongs to my longtime friend Mary Robbins, who helped me focus my thoughts and see things from a different perspective. And to Nathalie Farman-Farma for her encouragement and progress check-ins, reminding me of our shared former days of concurrent thesis writing (and Al Forno self-treating) at Brown.

I can't imagine I ever would have been able to do a book in the first place without the generous support of the editors who have published my work over the years, whom I thank in my first book. For those who have continued since then, I wish first to thank the lovely and kind Amy Astley for the privilege of having my projects, including two of my own homes, featured in *Architectural Digest*, and, together with Margaret Russell, for the repeated recognition and high honor of being named to the AD100.

I thank Michael Boodro, Sophie Dow, Clinton Smith, Newell Turner, Whitney Robinson, Steele Marcoux, Samuel Cochran, Howard Christian, Robert Rufino, Mitchell Owens, and Shax Riegler for all their efforts in the various stories for *AD*, *Elle Decor*, *House Beautiful*, and *Veranda*. And, to Jacqueline Terrebonne for the honor of publishing my favorite London project in her first issue as editor in chief at *Galerie*. I very much want to thank the glamorous and savvy Martina Mondadori for her friendship and for including us in her American issue, making James and me a part of the big *Cabana* family.

Major thanks to dearest Senga Mortimer for her continued mentorship, advice, and friendship. There isn't a project I do that I don't want to show her my every thought and idea to discuss and learn.

Of course, I owe a huge debt of gratitude to my clients, who entrusted me to work on their extraordinary homes and allowed me to show that work. I will always be grateful to them, especially those with whom I have collaborated for so many years on multiple projects. To Alex and Eliza Bolen, Hamilton South, and Annette de la Renta, thank you for suggesting me to help with the refreshing of Oscar's perfect design of Tortuga Bay in the Dominican Republic. And to Haydee and Frank Rainieri and their family for trusting me and for making my first commercial project such a pleasure.

No design would be possible without all the craftsmen and artisans who help me see things through, but there are those to whom I give special thanks for going the extra distance for me over the years: Gregory Gurfein, Joe Calagna and everyone at Anthony Lawrence Belfair, Shahram Nazar, Agustin Hurtado, Cheryl Fitzpatrick and Paul Boyko, Brian Kehoe, Frank Floria, Gilded Moon Framing, S. Donadic, Dean Fine Building, INS Contractors, Holmes Hole Builders, BTC Builders Inc, Hamilton Hoge, Schlauch Bottcher Construction, Cottages and Castles, Wolcott Builders, Elizabeth Hargraves, Tigran Gulyan, Kay Neal, David Miller-Engel, Cecilia Garzon, JJ Snyder, Paul Maybaum, Dora Helwig, Garrison Rousseau, Liana Reyes, Ihron Barrera, Aurora de la Rocha, Alex Schuchard, Doug Haley, Jerry Kemp, Matthew Higgins, Victor Hernandez, Agnes Pisalska, Michele and Victor Guarneri, Andy Breslin, Ahmad Suleiman, Sandra Santos, Lisa Simkin, Eliot Wright Workroom, Rosenfeld Interiors, Metalworks Inc., Celebrity Moving, Pure Freight, and Aiston Fine Art Services.

Of course none of these projects could have ever been finished, let alone taken on, without the hard work and organizational efforts of my entire office. Zoe Brill, Jessie Low, Samantha Penner, Samantha Schacht, Eliza Crater, Lilse McKenna, Donna Irwin, Dorota Pyrek, Noelia Tarquino, and Sally Nepal. And, I especially wish to thank Michael Elfenbein for his architectural expertise and skilled hand.

Most importantly, I thank my partner, James Sansum, for helping me with every aspect of this book and our life together. He is the very best sounding board. I could not have done any of this, book or otherwise, without his keen eye, exhaustive efforts, and refined sense of humor.

Markham Roberts: Notes on Decorating
First published in 2020 by The Vendome Press
Vendome is a registered trademark of The Vendome Press, LLC

NEW YORK
Suite 2043
244 Fifth Avenue
New York, NY 10001

LONDON
63 Edith Grove
London,
SW10 0LB, UK

www.vendomepress.com

Distributed in North America by Abrams Books
Distributed in the United Kingdom, and the rest
of the world, by Thames & Hudson

ISBN 978-0-86565-385-6

PUBLISHERS: Beatrice Vincenzini, Mark Magowan, and Francesco Venturi
EDITOR: Jacqueline Decter
PRODUCTION DIRECTOR: Jim Spivey
DESIGNER: Celia Fuller

Library of Congress
Cataloging-in-Publication Data

Names: Roberts, Markham, author. | Hancock,
Nelson, photographer
(expression)
Title: Markham Roberts : notes on decorating
/ foreword by Alison Levasseur
; photography by Nelson Hancock.
Description: New York : Vendome, [2020]
Identifiers: LCCN 2020021849 | ISBN
9780865653856 (hardcover)
Subjects: LCSH: Roberts, Markham--Themes,
motives. | Interior
decoration--United States.
Classification: LCC NK2004.3.R624 A4 2020
| DDC 747.092--dc23
LC record available at
https://lccn.loc.gov/2020021849

Printed and bound in China by
1010 Printing International Ltd.
FIRST PRINTING

PHOTO CREDITS
All photos by Nelson Hancock, with
the exception of the following:
Miguel Flores-Vianna: pp. 2–3, 12, 19, 20,
22–31, 118–19, 122–23, 163, 171, 176;
Stephen Kent Johnson: pp. 4–5, 14, 17,
129, 190–91; Bjorn Wallander: pp. 10,
54, 56, 58–59, 62–75; Thomas Loof:
pp. 116, 154–55, 181, 200–3

CASE: Detail of Scalamandré's
Cork Illusions/ French
Mosaic wall covering.
THIS PAGE: A large-scale paisley
print upholsters the walls in
this Los Angeles guest room,
furnished with an important
Deco amboyna chest and a mirror
with a penwork-decorated bone
frame in which a Vic Muniz
collage photograph is reflected.